The Many Faces of Edward Sherriff Curtis

The Many Faces of Edward Sherriff Curtis

Portraits and Stories from Native North America

Steadman Upham *and* Nat Zappia

Photography by
Edward Sherriff Curtis

Printmaking by
Steve Schenck and Rani Tagland

The Gilcrease Museum *and the* Thomas Gilcrease Association • *Tulsa*
in association with
University of Washington Press • *Seattle, London*

Editorial services and project
management by Suzanne G. Fox,
Red Bird Publishing, Inc.,
Bozeman, Montana
Graphic design by Carol Beehler,
Bethesda, Maryland
Printed by Dual Graphics,
Brea, California

GILCREASE MUSEUM
1400 North Gilcrease Museum Road
Tulsa, Oklahoma 74127-2100
www.gilcrease.org

UNIVERSITY OF WASHINGTON PRESS
PO Box 50096
Seattle, Washington 98145-5096
www.washington.edu/uwpress

Library of Congress
Cataloging-in-Publication Data

Curtis, Edward S., 1868–1952.
The many faces of Edward Sherriff Curtis:
portraits and stories from Native North
America / by Steadman Upham and Nat
Zappia; photography by Edward Sherriff
Curtis; printmaking by Stephen Schenk and
Rani Tagland.
    p. cm.
ISBN 0-295-98625-5 (hardback: alk. paper)
ISBN 0-295-98626-3 (pbk.: alk. paper)
1. Indians of North America — Portraits.
2. Indians of North America — History.
I. Upham, Steadman. II. Zappia, Nat.
III. Title.
E89.C875 2006
970.004'97 — dc22   2006004086

Right: *Canyon de Chelly*
Page 1: *Waihusiwa — a Zuni Kyaqimassi*
(detail)
Frontispiece: *Why Wn Se Wa*
Front cover: *A Young Mother — Taos* (detail)
Back cover: *Okuwa-tsu (Cloud Yellow) —
San Ildefonso* (detail)

Contents

THIS BOOK is part of a longer-term project undertaken by The Capital Group Foundation that is designed to bring the photographic art of Edward Sherriff Curtis to a new generation of viewers. The several individuals involved in the project came to it in quite different ways. Steadman Upham's participation began more than five years ago, when he met with two directors of The Capital Group Foundation, Robert Egelston and Robbie Macfarlane. They were pondering a very interesting proposition. The foundation directors had become acquainted with a direct lineal descendant of Edward Sherriff[1] Curtis who was in possession of several hundred original Curtis glass negatives, nitrate cellulose film images, and unpublished prints. At first, this individual was reluctant to let us disclose his identity to those beyond our immediate circle. As a result, when Upham, Egleston, and Macfarlane discussed this project with others, they referred to this individual simply as "our friend." Subsequently, however, our friend agreed to let us disclose his identity. He is Jim Graybill, the last surviving grandson of Edward Curtis. Jim Graybill, along with his wonderful wife Carol, have been partners in this endeavor from the beginning, and we are grateful for their willingness to open their archives of Edward Curtis to us.

Initially, Egelston and Macfarlane had worked with Jim Graybill to determine if prints could still be made from Curtis' original glass negatives. Much of the equipment needed to print from the large glass negatives was not readily available, but over many months and a few false starts, several prints were finally made. Both the power and the beauty of these prints prompted Egelston to wonder if the foundation might print additional images to create a new documentary record of Edward Curtis' work.

After much discussion and mounting excitement, the decision was made to undertake this project. Macfarlane agreed to work with Jim Graybill to select fifty glass negatives from which prints could be made. Later, Upham and Macfarlane examined the prints in a warehouse located in a crowded industrial neighborhood on the southeast side of Los Angeles. There, they poured over dozens of prints for the better part of an afternoon, awestruck by the sheer artistry and deep ethnographic content of Curtis' work.

In the interim, Egelston, Macfarlane, and Upham engaged in several deep and long conversations about this project. These conversations were enriched and broadened by the participation of Martha Williams, director and curatorial consultant to The Capital Group Foundation. Upham was involved because at the time he was serving as president of Claremont Graduate University (CGU). CGU is a steward of The Capital Group Foundation's contemporary art collection and, if the project went forward, Egelston and Macfarlane wanted to extend the foundation's relationship with CGU to include the Curtis photographic materials. Upham is also a professor of archaeology and anthropology whose interests in Native America had been shaped by years of fieldwork, teaching, and research in the American West. The convergence of administrative and academic duties around the Curtis materials was thus a happy and useful coincidence.

While Macfarlane identified the appropriate negatives with the Graybills, Upham was asked to assemble a group of scholars to convene a symposium in the fall of 2000 that would examine the scope and breadth of Curtis' work. Like any good university president, he delegated this responsibility to people far more competent. Fortunately, the outstanding efforts of Vice Provost Teresa Shaw, Professor of History Janet Farrell Brodie, and history graduate student Sara Patterson resulted in a stellar lineup of Curtis scholars, including Mick Gidley, Hartman and Tsianina Lomawaima, Anne Makepeace, Alan Trachtenberg, J. David Sapir, Patricia Erikson, John J. Bodlinger, Pauline Turner Strong, Michael Duty, Gerald Vizenor, Ira Jacknis, Sally Stein, and James Faris. These scholars gathered for a two-day symposium titled "Visual Representation and Cultural History: The Edward S. Curtis Photographs of North American Indians." At the conclusion of the symposium, the exhibition featuring the fifty-one Curtis prints opened in the Peggy Phelps Gallery on CGU's campus in Claremont, California. The photographic prints had been made by Rani Tagland and the exhibition was curated by Dean DeCocker.

The original fifty-one prints selected by Macfarlane were representative of the vast number of photographs that Curtis made between 1900 and 1927. The prints documented many different Native American tribes west of the Mississippi River. More than half the images were of landscapes or depicted living situations, but twenty-three were hauntingly beautiful portraits of individuals from different tribes. It was in these latter images that we found the organizing principle for this book.

The success of the first project had stimulated Egelston to wonder if more might be done with the collections of our friend. He organized another meeting with Macfarlane, Williams, and Upham to discuss the possibility of making more prints from Curtis' glass negatives and nitrate cellulose film. Fortunately, the Graybills agreed, setting the stage for the book you are now holding.

Upham was asked to examine the Graybills' complete collection of negatives and prints and recommend to the foundation which, if any, of the materials might be represented in the second printing. As he worked through the material, he was particularly taken with the power of Curtis' portraiture. Among the more than 500 images he surveyed were portraits of individuals representing dozens of different tribes, people in all stages of life from infancy to old age. The sheer energy, beauty, style, and grace of these portraits convinced Upham that they needed to be assembled in a single exhibition, a single publication.

What followed from this recognition can only be described as a miraculous coming together of forces. Egelston and Macfarlane embraced the idea. More importantly, they agreed that The Capital Group Foundation would fund the printing of another group of negatives. The second printing would be devoted entirely to portraiture.

At about the same time, Upham met a graduate student at Claremont Graduate University, Nat Zappia, who was just finishing his master's thesis in American history. Zappia had been working as an intern at a museum in Los Angeles, where he had been studying the field notes and ethnographic material of Edward Curtis. In the course of his work, Zappia had discovered many stories and first person accounts collected by Curtis during his thirty-year field project.

Upham immediately introduced Zappia to the principals of The Capital Group Foundation, whose number had been augmented by a new director, Timothy Weiss. Based on the significance of Zappia's research, the foundation agreed to make him a research assistant to the project. Zappia's principal duties would be to conduct research and identify stories collected by Edward Curtis that would augment the work we were doing on portraiture. The stories presented in this book are the product of Zappia's research, and are included to provide a context for thinking about the world view and cognitive maps of the individuals depicted in the portraits.

Finally, we learned that because of other professional obligations, Rani Tagland was not available to continue making prints from the Curtis negatives. As a result, the responsibility of finding another printmaker and photographer fell to Macfarlane. Fortunately, he found master printmaker Steve Schenck, and convinced him to undertake the printing of the second group of negatives. Over the past two and one-half years, we have had the enormous pleasure of working with Steve Schenck on this project. We include sixty-three of his stunning portraits in this volume; the remaining seventeen prints are by Rani Tagland.

But this book is about more than portraiture. It is also about the people themselves, each one immovable, each one caught in a moment of time by Edward Curtis. While these individuals are "frozen" in the past, they are also brought inexorably forward to the present by the magic of Curtis' negatives and the printing mastery of the Steve Schenck and Rani Tagland. This past-present duality provides a sense of timelessness to the photographs of Edward Curtis that is only brought to rest by the mythopoetic stories Curtis collected. Together, portraiture and story included herein provide a poignant and unforgettable view of our collective Native American heritage. ✿

STEADMAN UPHAM AND NAT ZAPPIA

1. We have learned from Jim Graybill that Edward Curtis' middle name has been incorrectly spelled in many of the published materials about his life and work. Consequently, we have spelled that name "Sherriff," which is the correct rendition. We are grateful to Jim and Carol Graybill for helping us correct an historical error that is deeply ingrained in the literature, and to Robbie Macfarlane for bringing this important information to light.

A Context for *The Many Faces of Edward Sherriff Curtis*

"While primarily a photographer, I do not see or think photographically;
hence the story of Indian life will not be told in microscopic detail, but
rather will be presented as a broad and luminous picture."

EDWARD CURTIS, *The North American Indian*

THIS IS A BOOK of portraits and stories. Both come from Edward Curtis' monumental
documentary project on the North American Indian, a multi-decade undertaking (1900 to 1930)
that led to the publication of numerous books, articles, and folios of photographs and pho-
togravures. Curtis' books and images of Native Americans captured popular imagination when they
were published, but thereafter Curtis and his work fell into near obscurity. Renewed interest in
Edward Curtis and the massive output from his documentary project began in the 1970s in what has
become known as the "Curtis Revival." Since then, nearly as many books and articles have been
written about Edward Curtis and his images as he himself published during his prolific and quite
remarkable career as a photographer and documentarian. Our present project follows in this tradition — Edward Curtis made this book possible, but unlike many of the other books he inspired, this
one is not about him. Rather, it is about his subjects.

The portraits and stories assembled here are the product of untold hours of Curtis' labor
over a thirty-year period. His remarkable persistence in the face of extraordinarily difficult field
conditions and lifelong financial stringency has inspired many writers to chronicle Curtis' career
and to study his enormous output. Nearly all who encounter his work recognize his prodigious and
many-faceted accomplishments. Many scholars have focused on the man himself, revealing an individual driven by a powerful vision, single-minded focus, and attention to craft that only spring
from true genius.

Others have focused on photographs that Curtis made of staged scenes or subjects in elaborate (and sometimes culturally inaccurate) accoutrement. These critics have raised both the specter
of exploitation and the charge of zealous idealism in Curtis' search of a "vanishing" race and
"heroic" Indian. In our view, such charges ring hollow in the face of his entire corpus of work,
materials that constitute a substantial, significant, and largely accurate documentary record of
Native Americans and their lifeways at the dawn of the twentieth century. We thus find ourselves
part of a new generation of scholars who recognize Edward Curtis' lasting contributions. For the
documentary record he created, for its richness and texture as well as its beauty and its flaws, all
Americans, indeed all peoples of the Earth, owe Edward Curtis an enormous and enduring debt.

When we sat down to organize the materials in this book, we faced several significant challenges: How would the portraits be ordered? What underlying principle would structure the placement of stories? How would our narrative contributions relate to the broader themes suggested by Curtis' work? Did we need to connect the stories and the storytellers directly? More fundamentally, we asked ourselves, what deeper goals and purpose were behind the compilation of these materials?

In the context of such questions, we outlined and evaluated many possible frameworks. We discussed using the cultural affiliation of the subjects Curtis photographed to organize our presentations. Later, we discussed organizing the book spatially, by grouping the portraits in broad geographic categories — Southwest, California, Plains, Alaska. We even contemplated structuring the book around the chronology of Curtis' fieldwork projects. In each case, however, we rejected such organizational devices because they served to separate and isolate the subjects so expressively and sensitively portrayed in Curtis' photographs.

After working with the Curtis materials for so many years, we were convinced that we needed to portray both portraits and stories as a connected body of work, not as separate episodes, independent snapshots, or geographically disconnected events. And despite the enormous cultural variation evident in the eighty portraits presented here, we decided not to emphasize cultural differences. Instead, we chose to underscore the shared humanity and collective historical context of the subjects — that is, we opted to draw the attention of both reader and viewer to the cohesion, constancy, and permanence of Curtis' subjects and stories, not to their somewhat obvious and distracting differences. This preference has forced us to reduce and distill our experience in working with the portraits.

Our inspiration came counterintuitively. Normally, anthropologists and historians are prone to classify and divide a body of information, subdividing it into smaller and more uniform components that can then be compared. But because we wanted to develop a more continuous approach to the images, we decided to present the portraits in this book sequentially, according to our perception of the chronological age of the subjects. Using this principle, the order of the portraits was determined after we examined all the portraits over the course of a single afternoon. We spread all of the portraits out on eight large tables in the Michael J. Johnston Board of Trustees Room at Claremont Graduate University. We ordered and moved the portraits until an initial chronological sequence was achieved. We then began tinkering with the sequence, reordering and moving the portraits again and again. We did this until each of us was satisfied with the final arrangement. We make no claim for accuracy in this ordering, only for a carefully worked out sequence as we perceive it to be reflected in the faces of Curtis' subjects.

Certainly there is room for error in our ordering. But we do not believe any potential errors violate the basic premise with which we began, namely to reveal the unity and cohesion of Curtis' subjects by placing them side by side, just as relatives from different generations might align at a large family gathering. Thus, Curtis' subjects can be seen by the viewer as part of a larger, encompassing lineage of Native Americans, and not as remnants, examples, or artifacts of this tribe or that.

Similarly, we believe the stories are presented in a sequence that emphasizes the progression of life experiences and the universality of certain Native American mythopoetic figures like coyote,

OLD WELL OF ACOMA

frog, and badger. The stories serve two purposes. First, they dispel utterly any preconceived ideas about affinity, alikeness, or similitude between Curtis' subjects and contemporary viewers. Despite the intense humanness of each subject, despite the subjects' similarities to our own gaze and expressions, the stories tell us that these individuals had categorically different ways of knowing and explaining the world.

Second, the stories remind us of how history, beliefs, and values are transmitted in a preliterate world. The power of personal interpretation and the role of embellishment are evident in these texts, as are the personal spins on essential moral issues. Such a recognition is particularly important in the context of a book of portraiture, since the idiosyncratic nature of these first-person stories speaks precisely to the role of the individual and to the grace of personal expression. Nothing is so intimate and expressive as a photographic portrait that captures one's visage and "being" in a single instant; nothing is so personal and privileged as the telling of a story that illustrates the values and beliefs deemed essential for keeping the fabric of society intact. Through the art and chemistry of photographic printing and the contrivance of literacy, we can now penetrate this intimacy and participate in both that single photographic instant and the personal retelling of stories that would have been lost in the deep history of preliterate societies. In this sense, Curtis' portraits and stories become timeless, enduring, and constant.

NATURE'S BLOSSOM

It has been said that portraiture is always art,[1] and certainly this is valid in the case of Edward Curtis' portraits. Each has an appreciable aesthetic quality, historical context, and identity as a made object. Moreover, Curtis' portraits are part of the broader realm of human endeavor devoted to imitating, supplementing, and altering the work of nature — features that define our present understanding of art. But the images are also more, because they provide cultural, biological, and historical information that can be studied independently. The sheer number of images that Curtis made during his career (estimated at more than 40,000) magnifies the potential for scholarship in these latter areas.

The portraits, however, provide only partial information. The still countenance of each subject belies the fact that each individual is a living, breathing, sentient being who was part of an active social network. The photographs, of course, attenuate these networks — we only see one person at a time, and cannot appreciate the larger social context of these subjects' lives. Similarly, each subject is tied to the specific cultural and historical circumstances of space and time. Edward Curtis "invaded" these dimensions to capture the images, sometimes returning to the same group ten times or more to document what he believed to be the essence of the living situation. During each visit, Curtis photographed different individuals, to memorialize their presence and provide a kind of living record of the group.

When viewing Curtis' portraits, we are forced to confront two distinct qualities: likeness and identity. Likeness is a highly subjective quality, and is often based on stereotypical perceptions of the way people look or dress. For example, students of these images can easily discern the cultural affiliation of different subjects — San Juan, Zuni, Taos, Apache, Pomo, Paviotso, Yokut, Diegueño, Noatak, and so on — based on dress, hairstyle, ornamentation, and (in some cases) background. Thus, "likeness" steers the viewer to certain set interpretations held in the mind's eye. Identity, on the other hand, is based on a person's factual aspects — his or her name, place and date of birth, and kin relations. In general, Curtis' portraits are very "long" on likeness and disappointingly "short" on identity. Certainly that is the case with these portraits.

Biographical information on the identity of Curtis' subjects is almost nonexistent. In many cases, we have only a rudimentary designation — the subject's name, cultural group, gender, or some combination thereof (e.g., Old Ukiah Pomo, Zuni Man, Cheyenne Woman). As a result, we are driven to other interpretive domains to understand and appreciate the portraits.

To complicate matters of identification and likeness, the gender of Curtis' subjects is often obscured by ambiguous posing, traditional hairstyles, dress, accoutrements, or the proportion of the body represented in the image. We have come to call this remarkable feature of Curtis' portraits "silent gender." At first, we were frustrated by the pervasive effect of silent gender because of our passion for conclusive and precise data driven by years of training in anthropology and history. But as we have worked with these images, we have come to view the quality of silent gender as fundamental to the power, allure, and beauty of Curtis' portraits. It is not the maleness or femaleness of the subjects that matters, it is their humanity. In our view, the quality of silent gender boosts the viewer's appreciation of each subject's bold humanity, captured in such an enduring manner by the camera.

The quality of silent gender also leads the viewer to conclude that Curtis' portraits are not and should not be easy to explain, because there is nothing easy about what they represent. At the time most of these photographs were taken, Curtis' subjects were not yet recognized as American citizens by the government of the United States. Citizenship was granted to Native Americans in 1924 by an act of Congress, a recognition that followed hundreds of years of colonization and enslavement by successive waves of Europeans and Americans.

At about the time that Edward Curtis began his monumental project on the North American Indian, U.S. policy toward Native Americans had begun to change and crystallize. Passage of the Dawes Severalty Act, or General Allotment Act of 1887, was the embodiment of this new policy, which broke up reservations and doled out reservation land to individuals. Prior to the Dawes Act, U.S. policy toward Native Americans was based on the concept of "dependent domestic nations" articulated so forcefully by Chief Justice John Marshall in 1830. As dependent domestic nations, Indian tribes were viewed as collectives with a quasi-corporate status. Tribes were given title to land, and tribal members were required to live on these lands, but the tribes' status deprived them of the right to formal political recognition. Tribes thus remained separate and apart, and were not considered political units to be integrated into the United States. In fact, the laws of the United States were deemed not to apply on Indian reservations. Therefore, whites and others were free to continue their aggressive push to take control of lands allotted to Indian tribes.

Between 1848 and 1890, the ethical and moral climate of the United States toward Native Americans was greatly influenced by a remarkable public debate over who built the extensive systems of earthworks, or mounds, throughout the Mississippi Valley. In 1848, two antiquarians, Ephraim George Squire and Edwin Hamilton Davis, published the first detailed study of the Mississippian earthworks, *Ancient Monuments of the Mississippi Valley.* In this monograph, they argued that a "great race of Moundbuilders" once populated the Mississippi Valley, and that these Moundbuilders were unrelated to existing groups of Native Americans.[2] The not-so-subtle message was that Native Americans and their ancestors were not capable of planning and building the elaborate and impressive earthworks.

Others took the conclusions further, suggesting that perhaps Native Americans were not human. Not until 1894 and the publication of Cyrus Thomas' thorough and definitive study of the mounds[3] was the Moundbuilder controversy finally ended. Thomas documented historical continuity from the past to living Native Americans, but despite this scientific proof, public views of Native Americans were slow to change. This sad chapter in American history fueled the aggressive policies toward Native Americans adopted by the U.S. government and gave license to those in the Indian Territories who acted outside of the law. As Robert Silverberg has observed, "the controversy over the origin of the mounds was not merely an abstract scholarly debate, but had its roots in the great nineteenth century campaign of extermination waged against the American Indian."[4] Edward Curtis, photographer and documentarian, stepped directly into this milieu.

Though often disguised in the rhetoric of inclusion, federal policy was designed to facilitate the dislocation of Native Americans from their lands so that white settlers could continue to expand west.

Though often disguised in the rhetoric of inclusion, federal policy was designed to facilitate the dislocation of Native Americans from their lands so that white settlers could continue to expand west. In the early part of the nineteenth century, President Andrew Jackson's political maneuvering led to passage of the Indian Removal Act of 1830, a law that mandated the relocation of all Native Americans to reservations west of the Mississippi River. Following passage of this law, thousands of Native Americans were forcibly relocated to reservations in what is now the western United States.

By the late 1880s, however, a desire to "civilize" the Indians was emerging, as were efforts to bring the Indians more directly into U.S. society. One of the major proponents of this view was Massachusetts Congressman Henry Dawes, a plain spoken Republican who was once quoted as saying that to be civilized was to "wear civilized clothes . . . cultivate the ground, live in houses, ride in Studebaker wagons, send children to school, drink whiskey [and] own property."[5] Dawes worried that the collectivist nature of Indian tribes was a major impediment to assimilation. He believed that tribal religions and tribal governance councils were too conservative and shielded Native groups from the realities of U.S. colonization. Consequently, Dawes wanted to break up the tribes so that individual Indians could be assimilated into American society. Ironically, he saw the civilizing power of private property as the means to this goal.

TWO LEGGINGS LODGE

CRATER LAKE VIEW

His views and political activism led to the passage of the Dawes Severalty Act in 1887, a law intended to foster the break-up of reservations and stimulate the allocation of reservation land to individual Indians. The law reads, in part, "the President of the United States . . . is authorized whenever in his opinion any reservation or any part thereof of such Indians is advantageous for agricultural and grazing purposes to cause said reservation, or any part thereof, to be surveyed, or resurveyed if necessary, and to allot the lands in said reservations in severalty to any Indian located thereon." The law goes on to allocate 160 acres to each head of a family, eighty acres to each single person over eighteen years of age and to "orphan" children under eighteen years of age, and forty acres "to each other single person under eighteen years now living, or who may be born prior to the date of the order of the President."[6]

The Dawes Severalty Act was hailed by whites as a turning point in U.S. Indian affairs. The act was often called the "Magna Carta of the Indians" by eastern politicians, but in Indian Country, the act was viewed as another in a long string of broken promises. The impact of the Dawes Act was compounded by new policies established by the Bureau of Indian Affairs requiring compulsory education in boarding schools. The U.S. government believed that Indian children could be more carefully and systematically "civilized" if they were removed from the contaminating influence of their parents. Indian boarding schools were typically far from reservation homelands, and Indian children were prevented from returning home in the summer. Native languages were banned in the boarding schools, as were traditional ritual and religious practices. Compulsory school attendance broke up Native families, and the English-only rule began the process of limiting the transmission of Native languages from one generation to the next. These impositions ripped apart the very fabric of Native society, leading to social and economic conditions still evident in reservation communities today.[7]

Indian allotment and compulsory education in boarding schools were enormously destabilizing, and caused significant and lasting disruption and suffering, but more changes and turmoil were in store for Native Americans. With prodding from Protestant religious groups, the Bureau of Indian Affairs worked out an imperious set of new rules governing religious practices that were set forth in the Code of Religious Offenses, an initiative aimed at eradicating Native American religions. With the complicity of President Ulysses S. Grant, Indian reservations were assigned to different religious denominations so that missionary work could begin. The Code of Religious Offenses sought to eliminate traditional marriage practices as well as all rites of passage and intensification designed to reinforce and perpetuate Native culture, values, beliefs, language, and worldview. In short, the Bureau of Indian Affairs' Code of Religious Offenses denied to all Native Americans their First Amendment rights to freedom of religion and expression that are guaranteed by the U.S. Constitution.

This is the environment that Edward Curtis entered in 1900 when he began his thirty-year field project on the North American Indian. These powerful historical tides and catastrophic cultural circumstances provide the context in which each of Curtis' subjects stepped before the camera. In part, these circumstances explain the sadness, anger, and bewilderment that appear in the expressions of some subjects. But they do not explain the happiness, dignity, grace, and even nobility in others, except by reference to the strength of character, moral courage, and spiritual depth of these individuals. We find this aspect of the portraits to be one of the most significant and meaningful contributions Edward Curtis made to our understanding of Native Americans at the turn of the twentieth century. Looking at the portraits and reading these stories some one hundred years later, we discover not only a collection of interesting material, but also a tribute to the human spirit that is the key to all of Curtis' work. This is the goal of the documentarian, and in our view, Edward Curtis succeeded beyond even his most ambitious dreams. ✿

1. Ludmilla Jordanova, *Defining Features* (London: Reaktion Books and the National Portrait Gallery, 2000), p. 13. See also, Norbert Schneider, *The Art of the Portrait* (Cologne: Benedikt Taschen, 1999).

2. Ephraim George Squire and Edwin Hamilton Davis, *Ancient Monuments of the Mississippi Valley,* Smithsonian Contributions to Knowledge, Volume 1. Washington, D.C.: 1848.

3. Cyrus Thomas, *Report of the Mound Explorations of the Bureau of Ethnology,* Washington, D.C. 1894.

4. Robert Silverberg, *Mound Builders of Ancient America: The Archaeology of a Myth* (Greenwich, CT: New York Graphic Society, Greenwich, 1968), 159–160.

5. Archives of the West 1887–1914. http://www.pbs.org/weta/thewest/resources/archives/eight/dawes.htm

6. *U. S. Statutes at Large,* Vol. XXIV, p. 388 ff.

7. Edward Spicer, *Cycles of Conquest* (Tucson: University of Arizona Press, 1962; repr., 1976), 343–367.

IN 1971, *Touch the Earth* by T.C. McLuhan marked the triumphant rediscovery of Edward Curtis' images of a "pre-modern" America.[1] Many saw in these images an America filled with virtue, mystery, and grandeur. *Touch the Earth* revealed a pastoral world uncluttered by the turbulent events of the late twentieth century. Perhaps more than anything else, the images in McLuhan's book gave Americans who were unaware of Native American history a reference point to reflect on their own time and place in the world.

Just as the images from *Touch the Earth* created a new avenue for reflection and understanding during the late twentieth century, so too did Edward Curtis' *The North American Indian* create a framework for viewing the world some 100 years earlier. Between Curtis' first major endeavor as official photographer of the 1899 Harriman expedition and his completion of *The North American Indian* in 1930, dramatic events, including a second industrial revolution, shifts in the centers of political power, and rapid expansion of the modern world economy unfolded on a global scale.

Many of these changes produced radical disruptions in Native America. Despite these changes, it would be a mistake to think of Native Americans only as victims. They were also individuals with their own histories, families, accomplishments, responsibilities, expectations, and dreams. Native Americans, indeed all Americans during this period, were caught in the advancing tides of industrialization and frontier expansion. Edward Curtis' photographs captured Native Americans in this "instant," and the stories he recorded preserve their words and world-view.

Here we will explore the global historical tides — the historical conjuncture, if you will — that washed over Native North America in the nineteenth and twentieth centuries in an effort to provide a broader context and meaning to the images and stories that follow. Specifically, we present a snapshot of global history at this time, followed by a brief survey of developments in Native North America that brought the Indians together with their indigenous neighbors and with other Americans and Europeans.

An underlying theme is the effect of the developing world economy on Native groups. The forces of developing world markets were pervasive and transforming during this period. Individuals were often powerless to withstand these economic changes and the social alterations they induced.

The subtle effects of these transformations can be seen in many of the portraits in which the subjects wear Western clothing or nontraditional ornamentation.

Native Americans were not alone in facing such challenges. Indeed, indigenous people all over the world faced similar assaults on their stability and survival because of colonial expansion, industrialization, and growth of the modern world economy. By using this narrative approach, we hope to provide both reader and viewer a better understanding of the times in which Edward S. Curtis documented so many different Native American groups.

A Global Snapshot

As we sat down to write this essay, we wondered whether the experiences of Native Americans during the nineteenth and early twentieth centuries were akin to those of indigenous people living in traditional ways elsewhere in the world. This period of history was marked by the rapid colonial expansion of Western industrial powers. As France, Germany, Austria-Hungary, Italy, Russia, Japan, and the U.S. expanded their reach into the developing world in search of new resources, they severely disrupted the settlement organization, social structure, and subsistence patterns of indigenous peoples. New markets were created and fed by goods extracted from the colonies established by Western powers. Cash economies were introduced, and forces of the modern world economy began to shape activities of both colonies and colonizers.

Between 1850 and 1915, the great industrial powers engaged in the "scramble for Africa" and the "great game" in western Asia, and forged an "Open Door Policy" in East Asia. Significant advances in communication (the telegraph), transportation (steam engines for the railroad and ship propulsion), medicine (quinine for malaria treatment), and warfare (the Gatlin gun and armor), helped Western nations remap the entire world. These innovations also bolstered changes in the patterns of investment and the sale and movement of commodities that greatly affected the ebb and flow of world trade. For the first time in human history, local economies in once-isolated regions around the world lost their autonomy to the emerging world market.[2]

The convergence of these economic, political, and technological factors produced a wealth of new opportunities, but also had devastating social and demographic consequences for indigenous peoples in different parts of the world. Between 1876 and 1890, many countries in the developing world — including Brazil, China, and India — experienced famines that resulted from stringent market regulations, severe droughts, and policies that encouraged the production of "export-only" crops. As many as fifteen million people starved during this time as grain for export passed them by on trains headed to newly established international ports.[3] The industrialized nations also suffered unintended consequences. Increased immigration to the U.S. and Europe brought with it the spread of contagious diseases, like the influenza pandemic of 1917 that killed 500,000 people in the U.S. and millions worldwide.

In India, a new nationalist consciousness was forged when once disparate Muslim, Hindu, and Buddhist groups found common political cause in expelling the British from their land. The Indian National Congress was formed in 1885, and successive battles for independence were fought

MORNING WASH—APACHE

against the British. Home rule and Gandhi's Civil Disobedience Movement ultimately led to Indian independence and the emergence of a democratic government, but only after a century of colonial rule and conflict.

China faced its own challenges during this period. The conservative Qing (Ch'ing) Dynasty was ill-equipped to deal with crop shortages and widespread famine. Significant social unrest developed as China assumed a "semi-colonial" status. Western nations with imperialist objectives took control of key Chinese ports to exploit and control the growing worldwide demand for silk, spices, and rice. These domestic and outside forces led to nativist rebellions that ousted the Qing dynasty, destabilized Chinese society, and spawned a nationalist movement.

To the west, the once-dominant Ottomans and the empire they created shrank under internal and external pressures triggered by rapid changes in technology and new political and economic alignments. Former Ottoman states broke free in an attempt to redefine themselves as nations.

Elsewhere, the abolition of serfdom in Russia and the Meiji restoration in Japan marked the ascendance of two new world powers. Like other successful industrial powers at the time, both of these rapidly growing industrial nations followed policies of colonial expansion. Both nations had designs on Manchuria and Korea, a rivalry that led to the 1904 Russo-Japanese War. Japan was the victor, producing a disastrous outcome for Russia that led to the Russian Revolution in 1905. Japan, on the other hand, had acquired stature as a world power through victory.

In Latin America, the growing pains of modernization were felt in cities like Buenos Aires, Rio de Janeiro, Havana, and Mexico City. Between 1880 and 1920, a Latin American export market developed that was based on coffee, sugar, rubber, wool, wheat, silver, and copper. For the first time, trade connected these localities directly to the world economy, and demand for these products in the growing industrialized world led to significant structural changes in Latin American societies.

Europe also shook under the weight of colonial exploits and geopolitical realignments. The major competing industrial nations — Austria-Hungary, France, Germany, Great Britain, and Russia — were forced by economic circumstances into opposing alliances to maintain political control over their colonies. Within two decades, these alliances collapsed and World War I engulfed both East and West. Perhaps more than any other event, World War I irrevocably altered the sociopolitical and economic structure of the developing global economy, and reshaped the aspirations of nations in a world that would be increasingly defined and dominated by a new "super power," the United States.

The efforts of industrialized nations to colonize much of the developing world brought an end to many indigenous lifeways and traditional cultures. Edward Curtis saw this change occurring, and was motivated to document both community and individual at this extraordinary historical conjuncture.

Historians have referred to this time of colonial change as the end of the pre-modern period, or the beginning of "modernity." Modernity is often defined as the large-scale integration of formerly isolated local communities into nation states, and the abandonment within these communities of tradition, native language, and religion in favor of individualism. This definition accurately describes what occurred between 1850 and 1915 in many parts of the world. Modernity ushered in a new era in which individuals, not communities, were the principal actors in the developing world economy.

Native North America and the Developing World Economy

The United States emerged as a major political and economic power at the beginning of the twentieth century. It was also at this time that the Western American "frontier" officially closed. Urban areas were growing, and the railroad had opened up previously isolated rural areas to settlement. Importantly, political and economic disruptions in other parts of the world led to a flood of new immigrants from Asia and Europe. New technology, new citizens, as well as new military and political imperatives, were changing the American world view — that is, the stories of isolationist innocence and frontier expansion no longer explained America's position in the world. Enter Edward Curtis.

Whether Curtis perceived he would be a change agent, whether he consciously organized his work to this end, or if, in fact, the result was simply motivated by his relentless internal drive and ambition, Curtis' photography and writing were destined to play a pivotal role in reshaping the American world view. Curtis traveled the West to create a documentary record of Native American life and culture at a time when much of the rest of the world was in upheaval. People in different countries were experiencing changes wrought by colonial domination. As in other parts of the world, the Native groups with whom Curtis worked experienced these global colonial forces unevenly.

There is little question that forces of modernity had devastating effects in Indian country, but different parts of Native America felt these impacts in varying ways. Each group's experiences depended on their geographic location and historical relationships with the people who lived around them. In many cases, such relationships reached back several centuries. Long before white settlers came west, virtually every Native American group had frequent and sustained contact with both their indigenous neighbors and with Europeans. In many cases, contacts with Europeans were benign and unintrusive. In others, however, Native groups were forced to deal with hostile armies, swindling land speculators, zealous missionaries, or the unintended consequences of acute European crowd infections like smallpox, measles, and influenza. Regardless of the specific circumstances of contact and interaction with Curtis, however, it is important to recognize that Native Americans across the West were already part of the emerging world economy.[4]

> *There is little question that forces of modernity had devastating effects in Indian country, but different parts of Native America felt these impacts in varying ways.*

On the Great Plains, groups of Arikara, Cheyenne, Crow, Hidatsa, Kiowa, Mandan, Pawnee, Sioux, and Arapaho traded, fought, and intermarried with each other well before the nineteenth century. Europeans eagerly sought access to these Native networks when they arrived, and they participated in borderland commerce that crisscrossed the plains. Such interaction produced an economic interdependence that was vital to the survival of all participants. At the edges of the eastern plains (upper Mississippi/Lower Missouri Rivers), French, Miami, Illinois, and Ottawa communities merged to create what historian Richard White has called "the middle ground," an interaction sphere that formed in the wake of interethnic rivalries and the expansion of European empires. White described this region as "a place in between: in between cultures, peoples, and in between empires and the nonstate world of villages. . . . It is a place where many of the North American subjects and allies of empires lived. It is the area between the historical foreground of European invasion and occupation and the background of Indian defeat and retreat."[5]

Within this middle ground, new political and economic alliances formed and reformed. The British defeated the French in the Seven Years War, but then lost their position to Americans in the War of 1812. Among indigenous groups, Iroquois dominance waxed and waned, while new Indian confederacies emerged to deal with different military threats and encroaching land squatters from the East.[6] Throughout these tumultuous times, the fur trade provided an avenue for subsistence, and led to the development of a quasi "common language" (a combination of French, Ojibwe, and English) that facilitated communication among the many different participants who trapped and traded over a vast area.

By the end of the nineteenth century, military defeats and over-hunting by competing Native groups greatly restricted the ability of the Plains people to hunt, trade, and seasonally camp. The infamous "Indian wars" of the plains and the policy of land allotment proved culturally debili-

tating. As with other once-isolated parts of the world, Native people of the plains struggled to redefine themselves in the face of a changing subsistence base and new political realities.

Great buffalo hunts ceased, but communities living on the Cheyenne River, Rose Bud, and Yankton Sioux Indian Reservations survived by farming, hunting, and fishing along the Missouri River and its tributaries. While many of the plains people Curtis encountered, including Marie Black Bear (Plate 4), Lies Sideways (Plate 15), Seery Alone (Plate 34), Oscar Makes Cry (Plate 36), Les Ping (Plate 42), Black Bear (Plate 55), and others faded in the face of modernity, other traditional aspects of life survived.

Indeed, for all of these communities, near-traditional subsistence living continued into the 1950s, when several federal public works projects, including the construction of the Oahe, Big Bend, and Randal Dams, permanently displaced villages from fertile Missouri River farmlands.[7] These three dams inundated more than 550 square miles of tribal farmland in North and South Dakota alone, impacting residents of the Standing Rock, Cheyenne River, Yankton, Crow Creek, and Lower Brule Indian Reservations.

The eastern plains were not the only "middle ground." Similar histories unfolded elsewhere, including the American Southwest, where interaction between indigenous groups, Euro-American communities, and the world market had a deep history. The structure of trade in this region was shaped by centuries of interaction among indigenous groups, so that by the time Curtis photographed Ohin Tsau (Plate 52), Charlie Wood (Plate 63), Why Wn Se Wa (Plate 65), and Star White (Plate 71), it is likely that each individual was connected to much larger regional economic and social networks.

Long before the arrival of European explorers, indigenous groups engaged in a vast borderlands trading network, running east-west from present-day California to Oklahoma, and north-south from southern Texas to South Dakota.[8] Meeting at established trading centers like the Jemez village of Pecos, traders from indigenous groups on the Great Plains traded buffalo meat, hides, and other goods for Southwestern pottery, turquoise, and obsidian. The Spanish quickly became part of this economy, providing guns, iron, and livestock to Native groups in return for food, slaves, and precious metals. By 1700, Native communities up and down the Rio Grande River and at other southwestern villages like Acoma, Zuni, and Taos established political and economic relationships with Spanish soldiers, missionaries, and traders. Pueblo villagers like Ahwasay (Plate 9), Satha Songivi (Plate 11), Coe Opa (Plate 39), and Ambrosio Martinez (Plate 44) were the descendants of those Natives who first encountered these quickly changing realities.

The numerous Native communities of the borderlands to the West (southern California, Nevada, Arizona, Utah, and northern Mexico) also underwent significant economic changes both before and after contact with Europeans. Indigenous trade networks of the desert borderlands thrived along several key ecological borders. In the southeastern portion of the region (Lower Colorado River-Central Arizona), Quechan, Maricopa, Yavapai, Papago, Halchidoma, and Pima groups supplied fiber from the yucca plant, pine nuts, mescal, mesquite beans, gourd rattles, rabbit skins, and martynia pods for basketmaking to groups on the Colorado plateaus and along the California coast. In Southern California, Mojave, Kamia, Cahuilla, Chemehuevi, Digueño, Serrano, and Yokut traders moved acorns, tobacco, eagle feathers, shell beads, salt, carrying nets, wooden dishes, and sea otter furs east from the coast to groups occupying the desert and plateau interior. Along the northeastern border (Great Basin — Utah/Nevada), Paiute and Ute groups supplied arrowheads, red paint, buckskins, moccasins, blankets, obsidian, mountain sheep skins, and buffalo hides to both their western and southern neighbors. These plateau groups also served as a link to the trade economy far to the east in New Mexico's Rio Grande Valley.

Throughout centuries of contact, each of these Native groups tailored its subsistence and craft production for bartering with trading partners in other regions. For example, a Ute trader meeting at an annual trade fair in the San Joaquin Valley would be prepared to trade obsidian with coastal Miwok, as well as grasshoppers to the Chumash. These annual trade fairs brought together peoples from many different ecological zones.

Because of the intense competition for subsistence resources, military alliances based on economic interests developed between groups.[9] Two such alliances were the Quechan and Maricopa Leagues. The Quechan League consisted of the Quechan, Mojave, Yavapai, Kamia, Chemehuevi, Hia C-ed O'odham, and western Tohono O'odham. The Maricopa League included the Maricopa, Cocopah, Halchidhoma, Hualapai, Havasupai, Kavelchadoma, Akimel O'odham, and eastern Tohono O'odham.

Groups in the Quechan League were connected to trade networks in California, while groups in the Maricopa League depended on goods secured from widely scattered areas of northern Mexico and southern New Mexico. The Apaches roamed this entire region, staging raids that disrupted local trade networks. As a result, many Native groups welcomed the establishment of Spanish military outposts and missions in Tucson and Tubac in the seventeenth century as a counterbalance to Apache raiding.

This competition persisted throughout the nineteenth century, as slave trading and livestock raiding proliferated across the region. As the scale of raiding increased, so too did the size and economic reach of the raiders. By the 1830s, the San Gabriel, Los Angeles, and San Bernardino ranchos were open targets for multiethnic raiding expeditions. Mojave, Ute, Anglo-American, Mexican, and even a few French Canadian traders took part in these large-scale raids.

One of the largest raids vividly illustrates the complexities of this economic enterprise. In 1839, an interethnic group of Mohave, Ute, and Americans numbering more than 150 made their way over the Cajon Pass in Southern California, and swept down into the San Bernardino basin. This group was led by Wakara, a Ute chief, and included the famous American trapper Thomas "Peg-Leg" Smith. The raiders stole more than three thousand horses from Californio ranchos. Using Mojave trails, watering holes, and hiding spots to escape, the group cleverly evaded pursuing ranchers. Many of the stolen horses were taken northeast into New Mexico, where they were traded to Santa Fe ranchers and merchants.

Although the arrival of the railroad ultimately destroyed such interethnic enterprises, sporadic raiding still occurred on the borders of recently established Indian reservations in the Mojave Desert and along the Colorado River.

Although the arrival of the railroad ultimately destroyed such interethnic enterprises, sporadic raiding still occurred on the borders of recently established Indian reservations in the Mojave Desert and along the Colorado River. By the time Edward Curtis photographed Monkey Face (Plate 72) and other Diegueño, Cupeño, and Fort Tejon villagers (Plates 14, 46, 53, 58, 69, 77) during the early 1900s, all but the youngest of them had participated in the trading and raiding economy of the region.

In the interior of central and northern California, the economic and political realities proved much different. Even though Miwok, Yokut, and Mono had trading relationships with groups to the south (principally Mojave and Paiute), they did not fully engage in the extensive and highly competitive southern trading and raiding networks. Consequently, Native groups living in and around California's San Joaquin Valley and along the foothills of the Sierra Nevada Mountains did not experience the recurring warfare that plagued their southern neighbors. But like all Native groups in California, these communities were disrupted by the arrival of horses and cattle in the early eighteenth century. While horses benefited trading and raiding capabilities (the Miwok and Nisenan particularly excelled at raiding), the arrival of European and American fur traders and trappers counterbalanced such activities.

AT THE WATER'S EDGE—PIEGAN

By the early 1800s, Mexican and American explorers began to disrupt Native subsistence patterns in the region as trappers like Jedidiah Smith and John Sutter and their parties encroached on traditional Native hunting territories. Unlike Native groups to the south, whose relative isolation in a harsh desert climate assured greater autonomy, the discovery of gold and the expanding fur trade quickly internationalized central and northern California. Some natives became miners or worked on large-scale farms in the region, but many Native communities were displaced and members of these dislocated villages joined together to form new communities. By the time Curtis launched the North American Indian project, many of these hybrid villages dotted the California interior, exhibiting a blend of interethnic cultural and economic values. Indeed, individuals like Jack Rowan (Plate 56), Old "Ukiah" (Plate 59), Su-donii (Plate 64), Koshonono (Plate 68), and Pavaish (Plate 78) — Yokuts, Pomos, and Paviotsos alike — ultimately survived together in hybrid communities.[10]

In the Pacific Northwest, a region defined by its bountiful natural resources, Native communities were also part of competitive trading networks. Chinook, Haida, Kwakiutl, Makah, Tsimshian, and Tlingit had developed sophisticated subsistence and settlement strategies over the centuries based on the exploitation of anadromous fish, especially salmon. The stability of the fishery allowed these groups to develop large, permanent villages and a complex social structure. Northwest Coast groups placed great value on the accumulation of wealth and status. It was in the context of wealth accumulation that a vigorous and prosperous trading partnership emerged between Russian fur traders and Native communities in the region. By the end of the eighteenth century, the worldwide demand for furs made many Native groups, particularly the Haida and Kwakiutl, extremely wealthy.

The wealthiest members of these communities commissioned the raising of elaborately adorned totem poles. Carving totem poles was a tradition that existed well before the arrival of Europeans, but the influx of new wealth from the fur trade fostered an extraordinary period of totem pole construction. Full-time, freelance totem pole artists began to move from one wealthy village to another. While these artistic expressions were clearly indigenous in style and content, it is a paradox that the contact with the broader world economy fueled their creation.

To observers like Curtis, totem poles were the most exotic icon of Native America. The animal effigies so intricately carved revealed a distinct set of beliefs and a worldview. Ironically, as he photographed these monoliths, he was capturing reflections of an indigenous world in the process of being transformed by the world economy.

In northern Alaska, Curtis encountered Native communities that he thought were completely untouched by civilization. The inhabitants of these villages, however, had actually been in contact with Siberian and Russian traders for decades. Native communities living on Nunivak, King, and Diomede Islands, and on the Alaskan coast traded whale blubber, oil, and furs for Russian goods. In particular, the Eskimo community at Kingigan served as an ancient trading center for both indigenous and Russian seafarers. Lying between the Siberian and Alaskan mainland, Kingigan appears on the earliest Russian maps of the region. While the people living in the far North undoubtedly lived isolated lives, they still brushed shoulders with the emerging world economy, albeit on its farthest and most desolate periphery. In fact, villagers of the region such as Jukuk (Plate 25), Nu'Ktaya (Plate 27), Okaiwik (Plate 30), Kihsuk (Plate 40), Tahopik (Plate 41) and

Qunaninru (Plate 48) may have been exposed to Russian Orthodox Christianity, and most certainly used steel tipped hunting weapons and other modern goods.[11]

The forces of colonization and the global markets they spawned presented enormous challenges to the cultural, spiritual, and economic stability of traditional societies around the world. Many indigenous communities in different parts of the world failed to survive. Others were transformed as they adapted to new economic and social realities. Still others resisted, making heroic efforts to preserve their language, culture, and lifeway. Each of these outcomes is evident in Native North America. Many cultural groups—especially in California—were unable to maintain their identity, and were overwhelmed by the advancing European and American frontier. Others changed and adapted—their communities exist today as reserved enclaves throughout the West. But none was able to resist successfully the penetration of Western culture, language, and values. Edward Curtis photographed Native Americans during this period of unprecedented change. The faces he brings to us today through his portraiture mark this moment in time and this unforgettable historical conjuncture. ❁

1. T.C. McLuhan, *Touch the Earth: A Self-Portrait of Indian Existence* (New York: Simon and Schuster, Inc., 1971).

2. For studies detailing the convergence of these technological, economic, and political forces on the global landscape, see Frederick Cooper and Ann Stoloer, *Tensions of Empire: Colonial Cultures in a Bourgeois World* (California University Press, 1997); Adam Hochschild, *King Leopold's Ghost: A Story of Greed, Terror, and Heroism in Colonial Africa* (Boston, New York: Mariner Books, 1999); and Daniel R. Headrick, *The Tools of Empire: Technology and European Imperialism in the Nineteenth Century* (New York, Oxford: Oxford University Press, 1981).

3. For an in-depth analysis of the devastating impacts of economic policies and environmental factors on the creation of the "third world," see Mike Davis, *Late Victorian Holocausts: El Nino Famines and the Making of the Third World* (London, New York: Verso Press, 2001).

4. For new approaches to native/non-native American history, see Daniel K. Richter, *Facing East From Indian Country: A Native History of Early America* (Cambridge, Massachusetts and London, England: Harvard University Press, 2001); and Jack Weatherford, *Indian Givers: How the Indians of the Americas Transformed the World* (New York: Ballantine Books, 1988).

5. Richard White, *The Middle Ground: Indians, Empires, and Republics in the Great Lakes Region, 1650–1815* (Cambridge: Cambridge University Press, 1991), p. x.

6. For an analysis of the impact of Iroquois expansion on the western frontier, see Jane T. Merritt, *At The Crossroads: Indians and Empires on a Mid-Atlantic Frontier, 1700–1763* (Chapel Hill: University of North Carolina Press, 2003).

7. Michael L. Lawson, *Dammed Indians: The Pick-Sloan Plan and The Missouri River Sioux, 1944–1980* (Norman: University of Oklahoma Press, 1982).

8. James Brooks provides an excellent overview of the region in *Captives and Cousins: Slavery, Kinship, and Community in the Southwest Borderlands* (Chapel Hill: University of North Carolina Press, 2002).

9. Mark Santiago provides an overview of the borderland region and its players in *Massacre at the Yuma Crossing: Spanish Relations with the Quechans, 1779–1782* (Tucson: University of Arizona Press, 1998).

10. For an overview of the native Californian interior, see Albert Hurtado, *Indian Survival on the California Frontier* (New Haven, Connecticut and London, England: Yale University Press, 1988).

11. For an overview of the Alaska-native communities Curtis visited, see Shannon Lowry, *Natives of the Far North: Alaska's Vanishing Culture in the Eye of Edward Sheriff Curtis* (Mechanicsburg, Pennsylvania: Stackpole Books, 1994).

Reflections on Edward Curtis and His Project

EDWARD CURTIS entered Indian country at a time of overwhelming cultural change, and it is in this context that the North American Indian project emerged to tell two national stories. One story was told by Native Americans and was preserved by Curtis in photographs, on phonographic records, and in leather-bound books. It was an extremely diverse, yet deeply personal reflection of Native life and customs that featured the Indians themselves. The other story was told by Curtis the documentarian. It was a heroic narrative dedicated to the vanishing American Indian. The former narrative would gain in stature, value, and importance only as time passed, while the latter story was embraced immediately by Americans living outside of Indian country. Each story is a vital part of our national heritage.

Curtis did not begin his career with the North American Indian project. Instead, he launched his career by gaining the position of official photographer for the Harriman Expedition of 1899. It was on this expedition that he built his reputation as one of the nation's preeminent natural history photographers.[1] This project and expedition also illustrate the convergence of larger world historical trends.

The Harriman Expedition was organized by Union Pacific railroad tycoon Edward Harriman. The party consisted of twenty-three of the nation's leading scientific researchers. This distinguished group included naturalists John Muir and George Bird Grinnell, chief of the U.S. Biological Survey C. Hart Merriam, ornithologist John Burroughs, geologist Karl Gilbert, and conservationist and chief of the U.S. Division of Forestry Gifford Pinchot. These prominent individuals traveled to the last great American frontier, Alaska, to catalogue an untamed wilderness. Ironically, this expedition occurred at the same time as the Klondike gold rush, a colonizing effort that would have significant deleterious effects on Alaska's natural environment and Native people.

The search for precious metals was stimulated by the second industrial revolution. The prosperity brought about by the expansion of industrial output affected all of the Western powers, but none so strongly as the United States. U.S. markets created an enormous demand for all kinds of raw materials. In the northern and mid-latitudes, precious metals were often the target, while the extraction of rubber and palm oil drove colonial efforts in southern latitudes. Investors like Edward

Harriman and J. P. Morgan provided vast amounts of capital to fuel this economic expansion, money that assured no region of the world was overlooked. Thus, the Klondike Gold Rush followed from the investment and market forces that led to mineral exploitation in many other parts of the world, including Southern and Central Africa, Australia, and Central Asia. There is thus an ironic convergence in the fact that Harriman, and later J.P. Morgan, would both serve as patrons for Edward Curtis, who labored to document Native peoples facing the onslaught of modernization.

As the official photographer of the Harriman Expedition, Curtis absorbed the scientific ideas swirling among his distinguished colleagues. His conversations and subsequent relationships with members of the expedition inspired him to undertake the North American Indian project. Using the reputation and contacts he made on this trip, he was able to gain the ear of president Theodore Roosevelt and convince J .P. Morgan to finance the venture. Roosevelt, Morgan, and other prominent leaders saw Curtis' project as an opportunity to construct a clear national narrative that illustrated "White progress." Roosevelt's view of history favored colorful, personal accounts that demonstrated the perseverance and rugged individualism of white Americans, something professional historians found then, and continue to find, racist and problematic.

In fact, professional historians at this time were in the process of dramatically changing the purpose and goals of "doing" history. Rather than merely chronicling and commenting on events, historians wanted to capture the "truth" through careful, impartial observation. This change was also apparent in anthropology, where new, more rigorous methods of data collection and reporting were being developed. For the first time, scientific objectivity became the standard through which historical and anthropological research was evaluated and legitimized.[2] It was in this context that Curtis struggled to share what he saw as a vanishing American legacy.

Reactions to Curtis' work illuminated the split between the older and newer approaches in history and anthropology. Prominent Americanists like F.W. Hodge (Curtis' editor), Frederick Ward Putnam, and Edmund S. Meany were vigorous supporters of Curtis and his project, but powerful figures in the field, including Franz Boas, George Peter Winship, and Frederick Starr, opposed Curtis' work, labeling it amateurish, unscientific, and unprofessional.[3] This latter group held sway in professional circles, resulting in an unfortunate neglect of Curtis' work by a generation of later historians and anthropologists.

In the midst of this controversy over the scientific quality of Curtis' project, a number of libraries and museums in the country decided to subscribe to *The North American Indian,* putting each in line to receive the twenty-volume set of Curtis' photographs. Many Americans were first exposed to his images in this way. What they saw were photographs that communicated the harmony and oneness of Native Americans and their environment. This was a message that Curtis delivered to a growing urban population in America that was estranged from the land and largely ignorant of Native Americans and their culture.

Curtis succeeded in capturing public imagination with his photographs. His images connected to the American ideal of an expanding and limitless frontier, and to the nineteenth century notion of the "noble savage." In Native communities, Curtis' reputation was much different. He was respected as an individual and trusted as a documentarian. Such a reputation may be partly related

AN OASIS IN THE BADLANDS—SIOUX

to the generous payments he made to the subjects he photographed. One of Curtis' first Native subjects, Princess Angeline, daughter of Chief Seattle (Plate 75), illustrates how Curtis approached his work. As Curtis recalled, "I paid the princess a dollar for each picture I made. . . . This seemed to please her greatly, and she indicated that she preferred to spend her time having pictures taken to digging clams."[4]

But his portraits also reveal a sensitivity to the humanity of each subject. Curtis photographed each person at an angle and distance aimed to reveal the subject's character and temperament. His portraits show not only the effects of sun and wind on a subject's face, but we also see the impact of history and the toll it takes on the moral and emotional fiber of the individual.

Unlike other visitors to Indian country, Curtis sought out and listened to the most respected storytellers who could share deep and accurate depictions of their communities. He placed great value on these stories. Indeed, as the project evolved over a thirty-year period, Curtis became more and more deeply concerned about preserving the stories of the people he photographed.

In every human society, and especially in preliterate ones, oral traditions and narratives are key to cultural survival. The stories pass on knowledge about social taboos, cultural and religious beliefs, moral values, as well as utilitarian and technological information (e.g., ways of planting, hunting, fighting, etc.). Faced with rapidly changing realities, Native American communities saw in Curtis someone who could help preserve their stories for future generations. Paradoxically, Native

Americans were suspicious of and reticent about embracing many of the technological changes sweeping across Indian country, yet surprisingly they allowed the new technology of camera and phonograph to record and preserve their images, ideas, and memories.

While Curtis has been criticized for "dressing up" Native people in his photographs, such criticism pertains to only a small number of the images he made. The vast number of his images accurately reflects the realities of the Native communities he encountered. For many Native communities, Curtis provided one of the few opportunities for Natives to convey the richness and meaning of their culture to an outside audience. When Curtis was among the Cheyenne and other Plains Indian communities, for example, U.S. government policy and the actions of Christian missionaries had forced religious ceremonies underground. Yet Curtis was able to document certain religious practices, while he photographed individuals in very plain dress (see Plates 13, 19, 23, 31, 54).

In California, Curtis photographed individuals from hybrid communities (Plate 33, 49, 51, 57, 73, 74, 76). In the Southwest, he sought out subjects from long occupied communities like Zuni (Waihuisiwa — A Zuni Kyaqimassi, Plate 38) and San Juan (Tse-ka — Cacique of San Juan, Plate 61). Curtis also photographed children (Plates 1–4) and adolescents (Plates 12, 17–18) in an effort to portray the full range and variety of Native peoples.

The stories collected by Edward Curtis provide another compelling glimpse into Native North America and a link between past and present. Curtis recorded ancient myths, lyrics from traditional songs, linguistic terminology, as well as recent events. Over the course of the project, Curtis supported the stories of tribal elders, even when their accounts put them at odds with the national story that the North American Indian portrayed. This happened, for example, in 1907 when Curtis and his assistants arranged a tour and investigation of the Little Bighorn battlefield with a group of Crow elders who had served as scouts under General George Armstrong Custer. Their recollections and accounts of the battle, which called into question Custer's military judgments, contradicted the official U.S. Army reports of the fight. Realizing the errors, Curtis presented a revised version of events based on the descriptions of Crow elders. Risking a potential rift with his supporters, Curtis remained steadfast in relaying the indigenous view of the battle. It was this information that stimulated historical reappraisal of the battle of the Little Bighorn in the years to come.

For many Native communities, Curtis provided one of the few opportunities for Natives to convey the richness and meaning of their culture to an outside audience.

Using the new phonographic technology, Curtis also recorded the songs and stories accompanying myths and ceremonies. For singers and the keeper of songs, these records accurately preserved oral histories without relying on potentially inaccurate translation and transcription. Throughout these reenactments of great real-life battles, mythical origins, and oral histories, Native people shared their worldview. Moreover, the technology projected a Native description of the world onto "civilized" society in a direct and unambiguous manner. The stories were preserved so that future generations of Native people could listen to them.

Although Curtis recorded many stories himself, some were translated and transcribed by informants such as Alexander Upshaw (a Crow working with Curtis on the Great Plains), George Hunt (a Tlingit working in the Pacific Northwest), and Charlie Day (a white trader fluent in Navajo working in the Southwest). In some instances, these informants had to coax elders for days or even weeks to share their accounts. More often than not, though, older members of the community eagerly reached out to share their knowledge. One can only imagine the majesty and eloquence of these orations, given over several hours or even days. Many of these interviews also became village events at which the community members congregated to once again hear a recounting of their history.

Several such stories are reproduced in this book. From a larger world historical perspective, many of these stories like the Yokut origin tale "The Creation," the Hopi account of "The Destruction of Sikyatki," or the story about the Hidatsa "Home Boy," echo universal themes reflecting a search for truth and a respect for trust and loyalty. Others reveal local origins and traditions particular to certain areas of Native America. Most were handed down by countless generations of storytellers. All of them reflect dynamic cultures constantly reacting and adapting to changes in their environments.

During the last 100 years, the narratives of all Americans, Native and non-Native alike, have evolved in response to a deeper understanding of the country's history. Edward Curtis and the North American Indian project have added much new information to this process. In Native America, many indigenous communities have incorporated information from Curtis' project into their ceremonies, oral histories, languages, and worldview. American popular culture is also beginning to face its darker past with Native America in the search for a new national narrative. Native American voices are increasingly part of the American consciousness. The collection of Native American images and stories presented here thus augment a fascinating, rich, and ever-changing story. ❁

1. For a survey of the numerous photographic approaches during this period, see Paula Richardson Fleming and Judith Lynn Luskey, *Grand Endeavors of American Indian Photography* (Washington, D.C.: Smithsonian Institution Press, 1993).

2. For a discussion of the emergence of these professional disciplines, see Joyce Appleby, Lynn Hunt, and Margaret Jacob, *Telling the Truth About History* (New York: Norton Press, 1994); also see Peter Novick, *That Noble Dream: The "Objectivity Question" and the American Historical Profession* (Cambridge: Cambridge University Press, 1988).

3. For a discussion of the pro/anti-Curtis alliances and the greater historical/anthropological context of the project, see Mick Gidley, *Edward S. Curtis and the North American Indian Incorporated* (Cambridge: Cambridge University Press, 1998); see also Mic Gidley, ed., *Edward S. Curtis and the North American Indian Project in the Field* (Lincoln, Nebraska and London, England: University of Nebraska Press, 2003).

4. Victor Bosen and Florence Curtis Graybill, *Edward Sheriff Curtis: Visions of A Vanishing Race* (Boston: Houghton Mifflin Company, 1976), p. 7.

The Stories and Faces of Native America

The Stories and Faces of Native America

The Native stories in this section are taken verbatim from Edward S. Curtis' *The North American Indian.* No attempt has been made to correct them for spelling, punctuation, grammar, or consistency of expression.

Origin Myth *(Hidatsa)*

LONG AGO THE PEOPLE came from under the earth by a great body of water far to the south. A young man in a vision was directed to the root of a tree that hung down from above. Having the gopher for his medicine, he took the form of that animal and climbed up the root, burrowing until he reached a beautiful upper world. He returned and told the people of the wonderful things he had seen, and they began to climb up, but when half of them had reached the surface a very large woman attempted to ascend and broke the root. There was great sorrow on both sides at this calamity, for the people that had struggled up saw no more of those that remained below.

Those now in the upper world had brought with them corn and beans and seeds of the squash and tobacco. On looking about they saw in the distance a herd of Buffalo and some Elk grazing. The men killed a few of the animals, but the Buffalo and Elk ate some of the people, especially the boys. When the hunters returned with the meat, a white Raven croaked to them, "It is bitter." This was because the animals ate human flesh, just as the Raven did. He First Made All Things was on the earth improving it and teaching the animal people new ways of life. He told the white Raven, the Buffalo, and the Elk that they were doing wrong to eat people, and he blackened the Raven with charcoal as his punishment, telling him that if he persisted in evil he would be destroyed. The Elk had fine white tusks along the upper jaw. He First Made All Things pulled them out, leaving only one at each side, and he removed all the front teeth from the upper jaw of the Buffalo.

He First Made All Things hewed a boat out of a log and painted it blue with clay that he found along the shore, and told the people to go into it, instructing them to cross the water and bring back certain beautiful shells that were shaped like a shallow vessel with a long lip. Then he gave the command, "Power that moves the boat, go!" When the people reached the other shore they found men, from whom they obtained many shells, paying for them with food, and giving them also a woman. They returned to their own people and left the boat on the shore. Children who had been playing nearby when the command was given said to the boat, "Power that moves the boat, go!" whereupon it sailed away and was never seen again.

For many years they moved northward, coming at length to a place where the earth was burning. Little Fox made holes in the ground, in which the people hid, and the fire passed over

STORIES AND FACES

1. APACHE BABE

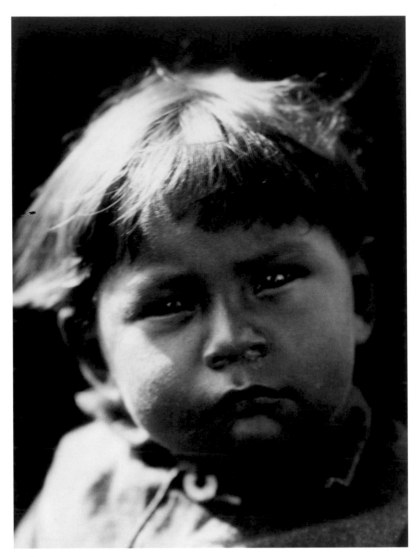

2. INDIAN CHILD WITH SHORT HAIR

X1811-05

3. Cope Vopie

them harmlessly. Then they came to a forest, and at the time when the grass began to grow a great snowstorm swept down upon them. After the storm had ceased they moved still farther north and met a people who spoke their language. With them they lived; then both tribes turned to the southwest and traveled until they were checked by a broad river, which they called Awáti. ✿

The Deluge *(Kutenai)*

IN THE DAYS WHEN THE PEOPLE all lived on the eastern side of Columbia Lake, they used to cross the water for huckleberries. One day, as they were returning, Duck and his wife were swallowed by a great monster, Ya-wóo-nik, Deep Water Dweller. Duck's brother, Red-headed Woodpecker, having decided to summon all the fish in order to find out where this monster could be found, sent Dipper up every stream, inviting all the fish to come; and Snipe he dispatched around the lake. Each messenger, whenever he stopped, called: "You fish are all invited to come! If you do not, we will dry this lake, and you will die!" So the fish gathered at the appointed place.

When they arrived, Woodpecker said to them: "I have lost my brother in this water. Ya-wóo-nik has swallowed him. Now you fish must know where this Ya-wóo-nik is. I want you to tell me where he is." Sucker responded, "I like to stay in the deep water on the bottom, and there I have seen him." Woodpecker immediately sent Long Legs, a kind of duck, to find Ya-wóo-nik, but the water was too deep, and he had to turn back.

At that moment there appeared in the council a very tall person, so tall that had he stood upright his head would have touched the sky. He was Nahlmókchi, and he was a person, not an animal. He had been traveling from the north to the south, stopping at each place to give it a name. Woodpecker requested him to drive the monster out of the depths, and the stranger waded into the lake. He kicked at Ya-wóo-nik, but missed him, and the monster fled into the river, up a small creek, and into the very source of the stream under the mountains. After him crawled Nahlmókchi, and built a dam at the place where the monster had gone under the mountain. Woodpecker now placed his brother, Sapsucker, beside the dam, and instructed him carefully: "When he comes out, say that Woodpecker is going to spear him. Then he will stop, and I will come round and kill him." Woodpecker himself then went to the other side of the mountain and kicked, and the monster started to come out. When he encountered the dam, Sapsucker, excited and confused, cried, "Sapsucker is going to spear you!" Ya-wóo-nik broke through the dam, grunting: "Sapsucker! I am not afraid of your spear; I am going to swallow you!" Sapsucker turned and ran, but just at that moment Woodpecker appeared, and thrust with his bill at the monster who, however, had started to enter the stream below the dam, so that he was only wounded in a foot. He hurried down the stream, leaving a trail of blood.

Woodpecker sent Beaver ahead to build a dam and stop him, and when Ya-wóo-nik came to the obstruction he could go no farther, and Woodpecker came up and killed him. He ripped the monster's belly open, and released Duck and his wife. Water began to flow from Ya-wóo-nik's wounds. His blood was water. It gradually spread over the earth until the people were forced to flee to the mountains. Still the water kept rising, and at last only one peak was left above the water.

4. MARIE BLACK BEAR

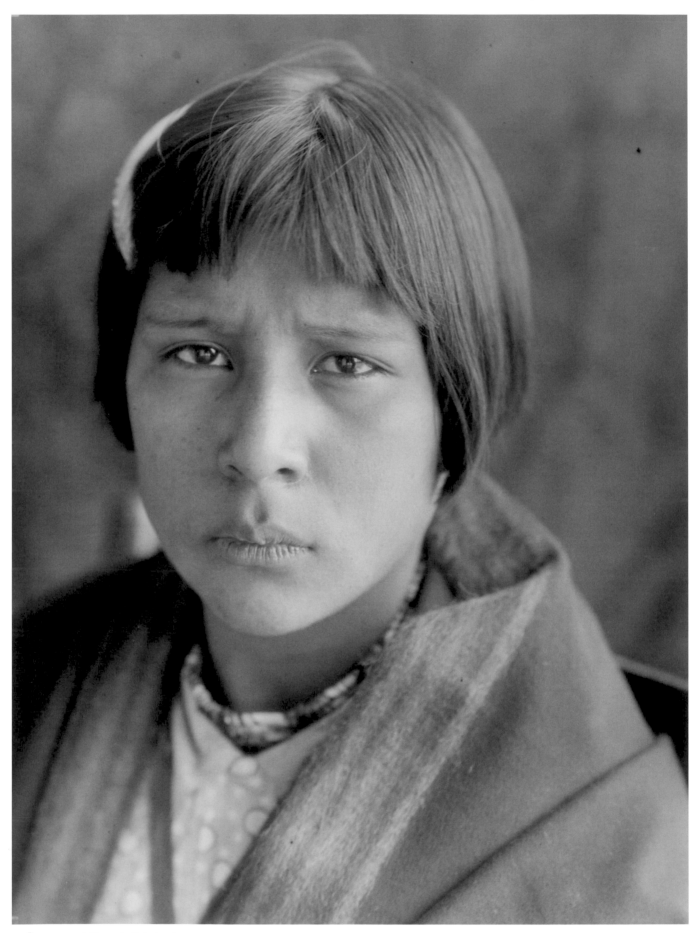

5. Indian girl with short hair

6. ZUNI PORTRAIT

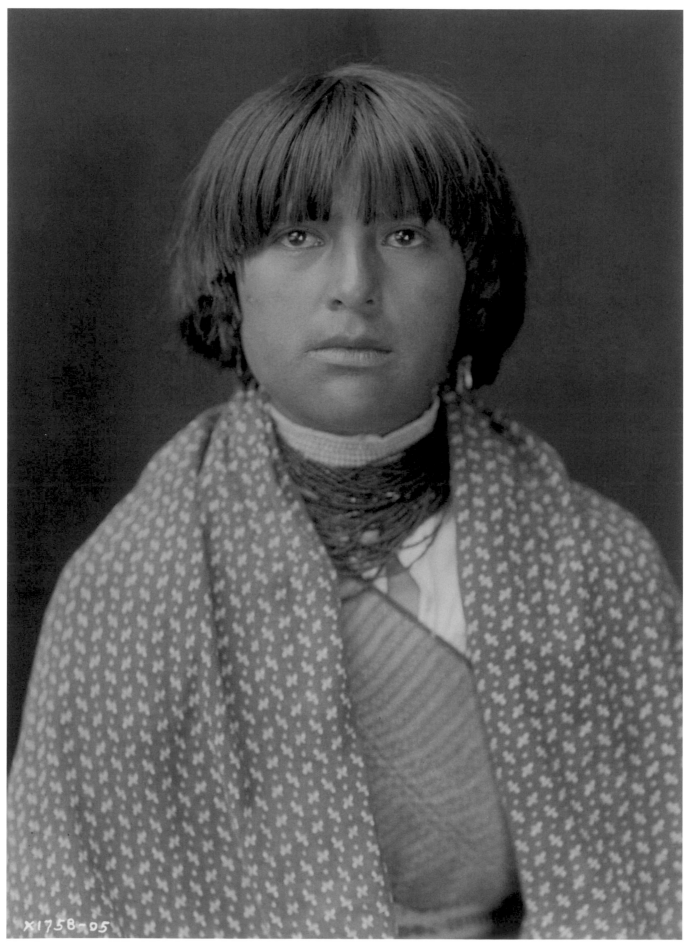

X1758-05

7. San Juan girl

Chicken-hawk pulled out one of his spotted tail-feathers and stuck it into the ground at the edge of the rising water. "Watch!" said he. "If the water goes above that last stripe, we shall die!" The water stopped at the last stripe then began to subside. After the water was gone, not all the people descended to the earth: the mountain birds began their life in the mountains at that time. ✿

The Cause of Lightning (*Wiyot*)

KUDIQTAT-KAQIHL HAD A SON. His name was Kudiqtat-kaqihl-kuwiliyawanaq ["above old-man his-son"]. They lived alone. Kudiqtat-kaqihl desired his son to be rich and powerful, and so he invented the gambling games. Then when the men from other places came and wished to gamble with the young man, his father would secretly keep saying to himself, "I wish that my son may win." And always his son was winner. He became very rich. Whenever he went hunting, his father would say, "I wish my son would get an elk at once." And the young man would kill an elk without difficulty. But he began to mistreat his father, who therefore shut up all the elk in the side of a mountain, so that the young man could not kill even one. And now again the men from other places came to gamble, but Kudiqtat-kaqihl would say, "I wish my son may lose." And the young man never won. It was not long before he had nothing, and he went away to the west. There he found Takak, whose work was to make thunder, and he remained there to help the thunder-maker. When very heavy thunder occurs he is unable to hold on, and is shaken off and falls down to the earth. He seizes a treetop, but it is not strong enough to hold him, and he falls to the ground, stripping the tree of its limbs on one side. ✿

The Creation (*Yokut*)

THERE WERE RAVEN [Hotoi] and Prairie-falcon [Limik]. They sent Otter, Beaver, and many kinds of waterfowl to dive for a bit of earth, but none succeeded. At last they tried Kuikui [a small waterfowl]. Down he went through three waters [three worlds of water] to obtain material for the creation of the earth. He brought up a few grains of sand beneath his nails. Prairie-falcon took these and worked them in his hands. He divided the material with Raven, and they went far to the north. There they separated. Prairie-falcon came southward along the western edge of the world, and Raven on the eastern edge, and as they traveled they dropped grains of sand here and there. When the grains struck the water, it bubbled and boiled, and mountains and hills appeared. The creators met in the south. People were then created by Nupup ["father"]. ✿

8. Unknown—Selawik girl?

X1708-05

9. AHWASAY (TULE GRASS)—SAN ILDEFONSO

Origin Myth (Washo)

TULI'SHI [WOLF] WAS THE CHIEF of those who first inhabited the earth. When they decided that it would be best if they became animals of various kinds and made way for a new race of human beings, Tuli'shi placed in a water-basket a quantity of cattail-down and seeds, and some grass. He set it aside and told the others to watch it. So they stood in a circle and watched it. A moon passed, and there was the sound of voices in the basket. They were indistinct. Tuli'shi poured the contents on the ground. There were people of three kinds. In the centre he placed the Washiu [Washo]; on the west the Teubimmuis [Miwok] and the Tanniu [Maidu]; and on the east the Paliu [Paviotso]. When the newly created people were seen, Kewe [coyote] protested that they ought to have four fingers like himself. But Lizard stood up on a rock and said, "No, it is right that they have five fingers like me." Kewe insisted: "They cannot do anything with five fingers. When I want to kill anything, I bite it." But Lizard declared that it would not look well for these new people to bite. They must use their hands; they must have five fingers. Kewe cried: "Do not make me angry! I will burn you!" But Lizard took refuge under a rock. Then Kewe secured the assistance of Mouse and went with him to the east. There were those who had pine nuts. He sent Mouse into the house where the cones were lying. Mouse carried them out, and Kewe ran away with them clinging to various parts of his body. He brought them home and asked, "What shall we do with these?" Tulishi said: "These will be for the Washiu and Paliu to eat. Plant them and they will become trees." So they planted the nuts, which grew into trees, and Tulishi told Matus [measuring-worm] to mark off plots of ground for each family. Kewe changed the original people into various kinds of animals. A great warrior became jack-rabbit, and his eagle-feathers became long ears. One who carried an ember wherever he went, to light the campfire, became sage hen, and the black spot of the sage hen's breast is a mark made by the ember. ✿

"Destruction of the Giantess" (Hopi)

I-TUWUFSI! PEOPLE WERE LIVING IN KISAKOBI. Pokan-hoya and his younger brother Polonao-hoya lived with their grandmother Spider Woman at Si'kpi on the trail that goes down the south point of the mesa. The two boys used to go down on the slope of the mesa to play with their shinny-balls. Suyuku [ogress] lived on the terrace. She used to steal little children, roast them in her firepit, and eat them. She had made away with most of the children of the village. Spider Woman often warned her grandsons not to go near that place to play. "Now, my grandchildren," she would say, "do not go over there to play ball any more, for fear Suyuku will catch and roast you, just as she does the little children from above." But they would answer: "She cannot do it! She will not be much of a person." One morning they started out as usual to play ball on the slope, and as they moved back and forth along the terrace, they gradually came to where the giantess lived. She came out and spoke to them, "My little grandchildren, where are you going?" "We are just playing along here," they told her. "Do not go very far," she said: "a little way from here there is a giant woman. You had better come in and wait before you go on." Thus spoke Suyuku. The boys went into her house, and she gave them mumus-piki and meat; and they ate the mumis-piki, but the meat they only pretended to eat,

X1652-05

10. A YOUNG MOTHER—TAOS

STORIES AND FACES

X1809-05

11. Satha Songivi

12. PO UH—SANTA CLARA

13. Young woman—Cheyenne

throwing it on the ground, for it was the flesh of children. After they had finished, the old woman closed the door, seized the elder brother, and dragged him outside. Already she had the firepit heated. But the boys knew what danger threatened them, and Pokan-hoya had already said to his brother, "When she throws us into the pit, you must urinate into it and I will spit my medicine into it." So when Pokan-hoya was cast into the heated pit, he spat his medicine, and when Palonao-hoya was thrown in he urinated. Thus they checked the heat, and were not destroyed. After putting them into the pit, Suyuku closed it and sealed the opening with clay, and laid fire on the top; and when the sun went down, she began to grind corn. She had two young granddaughters, who were sleeping when she caught the brothers. After finishing her grinding, Suyuku went to bed, and when all was quiet, the boys opened the pit and crept out. They went into the house, and each chose one of the sleeping girls and cut off her head and dropped the body into the pit. The elder brother threw in some medicine that made it red-hot, and they sealed it up and placed the heads in the bed. In the morning when Suyuku awoke, she called to the two girls, but there was no answer. She scolded them, but still there was no reply, and the children did not move. She came to the bed to drag them out, but found only two heads. Then she knew that the two brothers had done this, and she wept aloud, and said that she would never take another child from Kisakobi. Paiyasava! ✿

Yalali, The Giant (*Miwok*)

A MAN AND HIS WIFE AND HIS MOTHER-IN-LAW, and their little baby still in its basket, lived a short distance from the village. It was a season of famine, and the man remained out hunting late into the night. One night the two women with the baby were down beside the stream cooking buckeye soup. It was so late that the night was too cold for the baby, and the young woman decided to carry it to the camp and leave it with her husband. For she thought he must have returned, because a fire had just been kindled in the hut. A voice in the house said, "Give the baby to me." She handed the infant in, and a hand took it. But a long, claw-like nail scratched her, and in fright she ran back to her mother and told about the adventure. The infant meanwhile had begun a frightened wailing, and the mother ran back and said: "Give me the baby. He will not stay here." The child was handed to her, and with her daughter she ran to the village. Untended, their cooking fire died down, and Yalali, the monster in the house, perceiving that they were escaping from him, gave chase and almost caught them just as they dashed into the door of the ceremonial house. In the morning the people made a plan for getting rid of Yalali. They trailed him to his home and found him in a tree gathering cones. For when he had no human flesh he ate pine-nuts. They gathered brush and wood, and piled it around the tree, saying to him: "Gather here all the cones you can find, and we will bring the wood on which to roast them. We will pile up this brush, so that if you should fall you will not be hurt." When they had enough wood piled up, they set fire to it. Then Yalali came down quickly, and in desperation tried to leap over the fire. But he fell into it and was roasted to death. His body was obsidian, and when the flesh was burned off the obsidian burst and flew about in all directions, and was scattered among the tribes for the use of all. ✿

14. A young woman of Campo—Diegueño

X2710-08

15. Lies Sideways

How a Family Preserved Youth and Strength *(Nunivak)*

A MAN, WITH HIS WIFE AND WIFE'S MOTHER, lived apart from the village. The wife bore five sons, each of the last four births occurring as soon as the previous son was able to walk; but then she became feeble and unable to bear more children. Her mother said to her: "I am about to die. Bury me standing up beneath my head-rest and facing the entranceway." The boys, who had toy spears and bows and arrows, in their play used their grandmother's head for a target. When they reached manhood, all had kayaks. One night the youngest son, waking and having thirst, left the men's house for water. As he passed the women's house, he saw within a fire instead of a lamp, and decided to investigate. Inside he saw that his grandmother had come to life and was eating her daughter. In great fright he ran to his kayak and paddled away as fast as possible. He heard behind him his grandmother calling: "Y-e-e-e! My grandchild is frightened and running away from me!" Looking back, he saw her running through the air toward him, and though he paddled with all his strength, she rapidly overtook him. In despair he aimed an arrow at her, which struck her in the mouth; then she fell in the water and sank out of sight. The young man paddled all summer along the coast, and, when the ice set in, he abandoned his kayak to walk along the shore. Finally he came to a place where there were the tracks of many people. He found a pile of wood, and built himself a shelter. In the morning he was awakened by dogs howling, and heard a sled approaching, a sled driven by two men. When near, one said, "Someone has been here and disturbed our wood." The other, spying the young man, replied, "There is the person who has found our woodpile." These men, who acted friendly, took the young man to their village and clothed and fed him. He was adopted by one of the men, who were brothers. In a short while he married the daughter of the other man. Although he was happy, he often thought of his own village and family, and finally decided to visit them. After traveling a long distance, he arrived home safely and was welcomed by his family, who were glad to see him. He found that now his mother was young and well again, and that his grandmother was also alive. She said to him: "My grandchild, when you were frightened, you ran from me. You shot me before I could eat you. Here is the arrow which you shot at me. I swallowed it and have held it as a keepsake." Whenever anyone became old and feeble, the grandmother ate and defecated them while they slept. Thus they preserved youth and strength. The other brothers returned with the young man to the village of his adoption, where they obtained wives. Then they went back to their own village. ✳

16. Tohm-vio-ali-Tsay (down)

X1651-05

17. MANWELL TAOS

18. Okúwa-tse (Cloud Yellow)—San Ildefonso

19. Cheyenne woman

The Man Who Wished To Become a Medicine Man *(King Island Eskimo)*

A MAN WISHED TO BECOME a powerful medicine man, so that his fame would spread and that children would be named after him. He asked his cousin, a medicine man, with whom he was very friendly, to help him. The two were talking together one night at the cousin's house, when the man made his request. The cousin only laughed at him. When the village became quiet and all were asleep, the man decided to go home. Fearfully he said, "It is long after dark, and I had better go home, but perhaps a spirit might get me on the way." The cousin derided, "How can you expect to become a medicine man if you are afraid of spirits?" The man scolded himself for his fear, and asked his cousin again for a spirit, but was laughingly refused. The man, fear returning, asked his cousin to accompany him home, but the medicine man refused, saying: "I can see you as you go, dark as it is. I shall be watching over you." As the man approached the village, he was frightened at seeing something standing near the men's house. Looking at the person's feet, he saw that they were a short distance above the ground, thus proving it was a spirit. He mumbled to himself, " I thought something like this would happen if I stayed out too late." He ran; the spirit followed. He stopped; the spirit stopped. He stood still for a long time, and then thought, "If I stand here all night, I shall not live, no matter how strong I am." Again he ran, this time downhill toward the men's house, followed closely by the spirit. He vaulted the whalebone fence around the smoke-hole, thinking to drop through and thus escape, but the cover was fastened. He lay still on the smoke-hole, hidden in smoke and steam. He saw the spirit walk about the roof, and heard it say, "If that man really falls through the hole, I can not get him." Hearing this, the man jumped up, ran to the entrance, and inside to safety. Looking out, he saw the spirit standing in the hallway. An old man, awakened by the commotion, asked what was happening. The man answered: "What has that thing been trying to do to me all night? I am very tired from running. Please chase it away." The old man threw many things, but the spirit still stood there. Then the old man rubbed together a stone knife and a stone lamp cleaner. These he threw at the spirit, which at once disappeared, for these things always drive away spirits. The man never again tried to become a medicine man. ✿

Legend of Home Boy *(Hidatsa)*

IN THE DAYS OF TATTOOED FACE AND GOOD FUR ROBE, there lived in one of the villages near Heart River the son of Black Coyote. He was a handsome, well-formed young man, with long brown hair, and his beauty and elegant dress won the admiration of all the women; for his soft thick buffalo robe was decorated with eagle-feathers, and at the shoulders dangled pure white weasel-skins. From his lance, too, fluttered many eagle-feathers. While he was in appearance the ideal warrior youth, he had never been on the warpath. He would stroll through the village singing, or perhaps climb to the top of his father's lodge to gaze upon the young women as they passed. His actions were so peculiar as to bring upon him the ridicule of the men, for it seemed to them that he should desire to win honors in strife, and on account of his reluctance to join the warriors he was derisively called Home Boy. On the south side of Heart River, where it emerges from the hills and

20. A Zuni governor

21. A San Juan man

flows across the valley, rises a high butte. Men would often go there to fast, but never stayed more than a day or two, for something in that place seemed to frighten them. One day Black Coyote called his son to him and said: "You have no deeds; you are nothing. It is time you distinguished yourself in some manner, for you are a strong young man. Go up on that hill and fast for a time; perhaps the spirits will help you." So Home Boy went to the hill and stood upon its summit, crying to the spirits. During the night he heard sounds as though the enemy were coming. He could almost feel the ground tremble under their horses' hoofs, and terrified he fled back to the village. In the morning the people went to the hill to verify his story, but they saw no broken ground or trampled grass. His father said: "You are a coward! What do you suppose people will think of you if you always remain in the village, doing nothing? Tonight you must go to the hill again, and stay there no matter what happens." So Home Boy went again to the hill and cried. Again he heard the enemy coming, and, turning, seemed to see a party of mounted warriors charging upon him. The one in advance discharged an arrow, which pierced him, and as he fell the others swept by and struck him with their coup-sticks. Then the spirits promised Home Boy that he should kill many enemies and count many coups. He returned to the village in the morning. Shortly afterward the village was attacked by the Sioux, but Home Boy took no part in the battle; at night, however, after the enemy had withdrawn, he went out and dragged the bodies of their slain into a row. Taking the eagle-feathers from his lance he laid one on the dead body of each warrior, and said, "Here is something for you to take on your long journey." Then he lay down in the middle of the row. In a vision as he slept there the spirits of the dead came and told him to arise and to be not afraid, for they were to make great medicine for him. One of the warriors then took his bow and shot his arrows through Home Boy. This made him invulnerable. But when war parties formed, Home Boy still remained behind, and the finger of scorn was ever pointed at him. One day he and his friend were sitting on the housetop watching the people assemble for the Dalipike. Suddenly Home Boy leaped up and said with determination, "Today I will dance in the lodge of the Sun!" His friend looked at him in wonder, for only warriors of note participated in that ceremony. But he went with Home Boy to the sun-lodge, and watched his sober face as he marched in carrying his lance. The people were at first astonished at his temerity, then they began to laugh and to nudge each other, saying, "Look, Home Boy is going to dance; he must be growing foolish!" He boldly stepped up to the bowl of white clay with which the warriors painted themselves, and with which they smeared stripes across their arms to represent the coups they had struck. Home Boy painted himself, and placed a wisp of grass in his hair, a symbol worn only by scout leaders, to represent the hills from which they had viewed the enemy's country. His mother and sisters drew their blankets over their faces and went out. His father said, "I have tried to rear my son from childhood according to our traditions and customs, and to make him a brave warrior, but now before all my people he has disgraced me." And drawing his blanket over his head, he too went out. The warriors sat in four rows according to the rank their deeds gave them. Home Boy with a wolf-skin thrown over his shoulders and lance in hand stepped into the front line, as though he had a perfect right to be there. As the warriors danced out of the lodge, making a circle and reentering, Home Boy danced with them. He stepped on the black stone at the foot of the sun-pole, thus swearing that he spoke only the truth; and though he had

22. A CHIEF OF THE DESERT—Navajo

23. PINE TREE'S WIFE

24. "Ta Pah"—Antelope Water—Taos

25. JUKUK

performed no deeds in war, he told of his visions, while the people all laughed at him. A short time after the dance a war party was about to start, and as they marched around the village singing, Home Boy joined them and sang with them. The chief said, "Young man, you always sing with these war-parties, but you never go out to fight. You are making us ashamed." His friend, who was one of the party, drew him aside and said, "You must go with us, or you can never hold up your head in this village again." Home Boy replied, "My friend, I am going. I shall not join you now, but I shall be with this party when it reaches the enemy. Four days from now you will hear from me. Procure some buffalo-meat for me, the muscles of the foreleg, the shoulder blade, the tongue, and an intestine stuffed with chopped meat. When you camp the fourth night, watch which way the wind blows and listen carefully and you will hear me howl like a Wolf. Then bring out the four pieces of meat, and throw them to the big white Wolf you will see outside, but do not come too near it. Say, 'Here is some food for you, Wolf.' Early in the morning join the scouting party and you will meet a lone Wolf coming toward you. Say to those with you, 'There is Home Boy. He has seen the enemy, and I have seen them second.' They will laugh at you, but do not heed them. Remember what I say, and do these things." The second day after the war party had left, Home Boy told his mother to make him some moccasins, for he wished to go on the warpath. His mother begged him not to go. "You have never been away from the village since you were born," she said, "and you will surely be lost." But his determination was firm, and he went out of the lodge, leaving his mother to begin work on the moccasins. When Black Coyote came in his wife told him of their son's intention, and the father replied: "Let him go. I have done everything I could to rear him well, but he has brought shame on our household. Perhaps he will die somewhere. It is well." The morning of the fourth day the son went to his mother and said, "Are my moccasins ready?" She gave them to him, and Home Boy said, "Mother, come with me until I ford the river; then you may return home." She went with him, and when they reached the stream, he leaped into the water and disappeared, and a moment later a white Wolf emerged, dripping, at the other side. She waited long for a glimpse of Home Boy, but in vain; and she was puzzled, but remembering all the queer actions of her son, she came to the conclusion that he had done something wonderful. The Wolf looked back once, and then trotted away. Home Boy's friend sat that night in the brush shelter feasting with the others on the buffalo they had killed, and he laid aside certain portions of the meat, saying, "This is for Home Boy." The others laughed, and said ironically, "Yes, that is for Home Boy!" Soon they heard the wolf-howl outside, and the friend jumped up, saying, "Home Boy has come!" and picking up the meat, ran out. The chief, who had brought his beautiful young wife with him, in the belief that she and Home Boy were lovers, now turned to her and said sneeringly, "There is your sweetheart howling outside." And they all laughed. When the young man came back into the lodge, the people asked, "Did you see your friend?" "Yes," he replied, "Home Boy was out there;" but they laughed at him derisively. The next morning when the scouting party went out, Home Boy's friend accompanied them. The sun was halfway to the zenith when they saw a Wolf running toward them along a ridge, now and again looking backward across his shoulder. The young man with the scouts said, "There is Home Boy. Whatever he sees, I claim second honor." The others smiled, and cheerfully assented. They saw the Wolf run into a little coulee, and suddenly on the rim appeared Home Boy, dressed in a beautiful war-shirt and fringed leggings. His face was painted and his hair tied with strips of wolf-skin. The scouts were filled with astonishment and wonder. In answer to their questions, he said, "Nearby is a large war-party camped in a circle. They are so close you had better return to the main body." When the scouts were some distance from the camp, they began to run zigzag as a signal that they had seen the enemy. The warriors came out and piled up buffalo-chips, and, forming in a half-circle behind the heap, stood singing and awaiting the return of the scouts. Home Boy ran at their head, his long brown hair flowing in the wind, and the tail of his wolf-skin streaming behind him. When he reached the buffalo-chips he kicked the pile over, signifying that he would count coup on the enemy in the battle. The warriors were amazed, and murmured in awe-stricken tones, "Home Boy is here!" He told them that a great number of the enemy encamped but a short distance away, and that they had better prepare at once for battle. His report caused great excitement, and the chief spread a buffalo robe on the ground and invited Home Boy to speak with him privately. "There are timber and water here," the youth told him, "and it is a good place to fight. My plan is to take warriors who are swift runners and strong. I will leave a number of these men at three points between here and the enemy. With the fourth party we will make the attack and surprise our foe; then we will retreat to the third body, and they will cover our retreat to the second, and so on to this camp, where we will make a stand together." The chief called a number of the older men and told them of the plan; they approved it. To Home Boy was given the command, and he started out with the best warriors, leaving the inexperienced men and the old fighters in camp. At selected points he left reserve forces, and at the last stop he told the chief that from there to the enemy's camp the distance was great. "I shall take only my friend with me," said Home Boy, "for the way is long and some of you might tire and be unable to retreat." So the two set out alone and reached the enemy's camp after dark. "Whatever I do," said Home Boy, "follow right behind me and you shall have second honor." They lay in the brush all night. Early in the morning one of the women of the village came out to work on a hide while the air was cool. Home Boy stole upon her through the grass and rising beside her pierced her with his lance, and his friend counted second coup. The death-cry of the woman aroused the village, and Home Boy said, "Start back as fast as you can, and after I have scalped the woman I shall follow you." Waving the bloody scalp and picking up the bone hide-scraper which the woman had dropped, he started after his friend, while the warriors of the village followed in hot pursuit. Soon his friend began to tire, and Home Boy said, "Swing your head from side to side, and blow like a Wolf." When he did so the young man began to feel refreshed. But his feet grew heavy again, and Home Boy said, "Put your hands in front of you, and lope like a Wolf." That again brought renewed strength, and when for the third time he became exhausted, Home Boy said, "Pretend you have a tail, and put it between your legs as a Wolf does when he is pursued." This gave the young man strength enough to reach the third party of warriors, where a sharp fight took place. Home Boy fought bravely, and went forward to meet a single advancing warrior, whom he killed with his lance, and his friend close behind counted second coup. Then they retreated to the spot where the second party waited, and another engagement occurred; again Home Boy killed an enemy, and his friend counted second coup. And so it was until they reached the main camp on the river, where, in sight of all, Home Boy killed one of the bravest warriors of the enemy. Here the

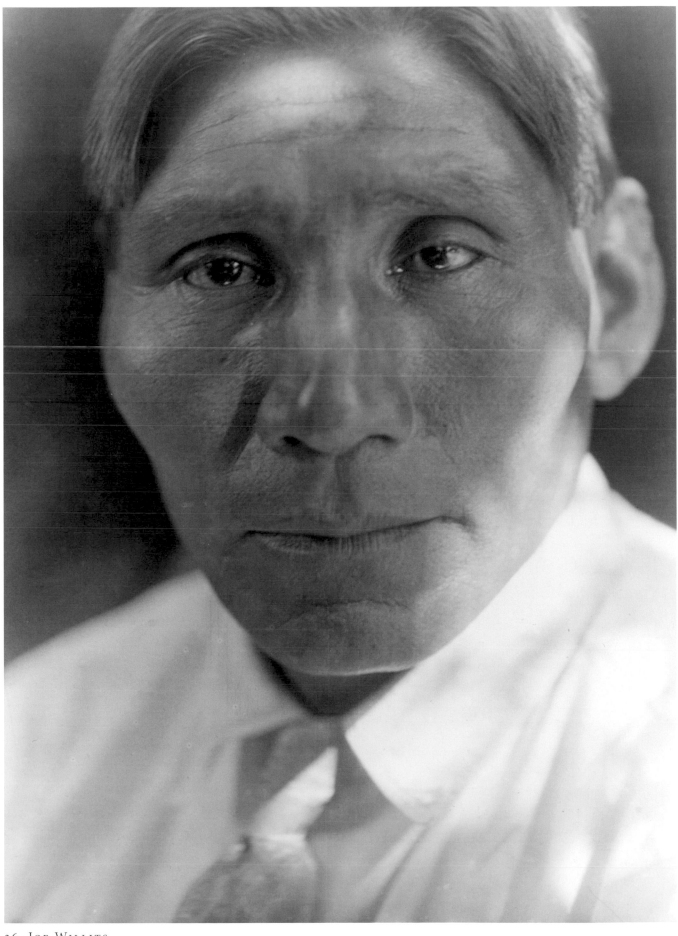

26. JOE WILLITS

27. Nu'Ktaya—King Island

28. HOOPER BAY MAN

29. A MAN OF TAOS

fighting was very severe, and the enemy were soon driven back. After the battle was over, Home Boy gave the scalp of the woman he had killed to the chief and the hide-scraper to his wife. The chief was ashamed when he remembered what he had said of Home Boy the evening before, and invited him to sit beside him, while his wife brought food to Home Boy and held a horn of water to his lips. When the war party started homeward, the hero told his friend that he himself would go alone. He watched the others out of sight, then started off and reached the village on the night of the next day, coming in while all were asleep. He hung his lance and robe where he usually kept them over the headrest of his bed, and lay down to sleep. When the father awoke in the morning and saw his son lying there, he said to himself, "I suppose he was lost in the hills, and came home after wandering about." But his mother, as always, was glad to see him, and prepared food for him, and when he had eaten he lay down to sleep again. Soon the returning war party was heard across the river. The people gathered at the bank, and some paddled across in bull boats to welcome them. They told of their triumphs, but above all praised the bravery and leadership of Home Boy. His parents heard, but thinking they were still ridiculing their son, covered their heads and went back into their lodge. As was the custom, the clansmen of the father came to the lodge and sang the praises of Home Boy, but instead of bringing out gifts as was usual when a young man had returned from his first war-party with deeds of valor to his credit, Black Coyote sat inside in deep humiliation. Soon an old woman entered and pulled a blanket from the bed of Home Boy's mother; another took a robe from the pile on which Black Coyote sat. When he saw these signs, he called in Home Boy's friend and said: "Is it true, my child, what these people are saying?" "Yes," he answered, "it is all true." Black Coyote's eyes were filled with tears, and he pulled the blankets from his son and said, "My son, tell me truly, did you do these things?" "Father, look at my lance," said Home Boy. When Black Coyote beheld the lance covered with blood, he was convinced, and knew it was all true. A few days later, when quiet was restored, the chief told his wife to clean the lodge well and to make it smell sweet with incense. Then he sent her to invite the young man, as he wished to speak to him. When Home Boy entered, the chief said: "Young Wolf, you have brought great honor to me. You scalped the enemy in the village and brought the scalp to me. All your brave deeds are good. I said that you were foolish when you danced in the sun-lodge, but I did not know your medicine then. My wife is handsome and good. She looks with favor upon you; whenever you come near she is pleased. Take her for your own." Home Boy replied: "Old Man Wolf, your speech is good. I fought that day to prove to you that what you had said was wrong. I killed the enemy in the village that your name might be in the mouths of all. As for this young woman, I admire her only with my eyes. I will come and eat with you and talk with you, but she must throw away any affection she may have for me. I will be a warrior under your leadership and help you in many battles. You shall be known as a great chief among us." Home Boy fought and lived for many years. He continued to bear the name of Home Boy, and it became a good name, for he won his eagle-feathers many times over. ✿

30. Okaiwik (Kingigan)—Cape Prince of Wales

31. Cheyenne woman

32. Oyaygeth O—Santa Clara

The Ivory Tusk and the Fish Belly *(King Island Eskimo)*

THE HEADMAN'S DAUGHTER REJECTED the marriage offers of all the young men in the village, because they could not pass her test. On her forehead she wore a long, sharp, pointed walrus-tusk. Whenever a young man entered the house to woo her, she lowered her head and pressed the tusk against him. None of the youths were brave enough to withstand the pain, so she remained unmarried.

In the same village were two poor young men who had grown up together. They were such close friends that they bore the same name. After much discussion, they decided that one of them should attempt to win the headman's daughter. One set out along the shore to find some weapon or charm to use against her. First he picked up a seal-bone, then he saw a fish. He asked, "O, Fish, have you something I can use for a charm?" "I have only a sticky belly." "What good is that?" "In the fiercest storms, when the winds blow strong and the waves roll high, I can always stick to the rocks. Nothing can tear me loose." "Will you let me use it for a time?" "It is all I have, but you may use it. Put it on yourself, and if a person touches you, he can not get away." He told his friend what he had, and the friend answered, "We are too poor to marry that girl, but I shall ask the headman for you." The headman was willing to permit the marriage, if the young could overcome his daughter. The youth fastened the seal-bone on his forehead, covered it with his hair, and stuck his forehead and pushed steadily. The point, resting against the concealed bone, did not enter his flesh, so he stood, disdainful and unflinching. They were then married.

The girl ran crying to her mother, because a poor youth had dared to win her when good hunters had failed. She was ashamed of him, because she was poor, and she refused to leave the house with him; then he pressed his shoulder with the sticky fish belly on it against her body, so that, unable to break away, she had to go with him. Now she began to respect him; he was too clever for her. When she chided him because he did not hunt, and hence was poor, he replied, "I can not hunt without proper equipment.

The wealthy father-in-law overheard the conversation, and offered a kayak and weapons. The youth became such a good hunter that he could harpoon seal from his kayak while the stern was still resting on shore. His father-in-law liked him so well that he refused the best portions of game offered to him. The youth's friend also came to live with the family. ✾

The Son of a Foolish Doer *(Mandan)*

THE DAUGHTER OF A CERTAIN HONORED MAN was as well known for her modesty and virtue as for her beauty. On a day when all the rest of the family were in the gardens, she sat alone in the lodge basking in the broad shaft of warm sunlight that streamed through the smoke-hole. Suddenly a shadow fell upon her body, and looking quickly upward she beheld far away in the sky next to the sun a black-visaged man, who made signs that he loved her. The girl gave no response, and after another declaration of his love the apparition vanished. This was Ohkinhedhe. In the course of time it was evident that the girl was to become a mother, but to her grieved parents she

33. KLAMATH INDIAN WARRIOR'S HEADDRESS

34. Seery Alone—Oto

X1807-05

35. Auto Somo

avowed herself innocent of any wrong. The child was born, but the women present were unable to discover it until, looking about, they saw a diminutive baby, black as a crow, dancing up and down in the middle of the lodge. Then it was known that the young woman was innocent and had been chosen by some spirit to be the mother of his child. The boy grew rapidly, and constantly moved about with quick, alert actions. Usually he left the lodge by way of the smoke-hole. One day he asked his grandfather to make him some little arrows, and when they were finished he desired a close-fitting cap of clipped buffalo-hair with a black eagle-tail for a crest. Thus equipped he would sally forth into the hills and slay many evil creatures. At length the spirits united in an effort to destroy this menace to their peace, and producing a dense fog so that Ohkinhedhe might not see the conflict and come to his son's aid, they approached the village. The youthful mahopini assembled the people in one lodge where they would be secure from random missiles, and went forth. Soon Ohkinhedhe's son returned filled with arrows, which he plucked from his body before going back to battle. Three times the champion of the people sought shelter to remove arrows from his wounds, and the last time he informed them that he could not return again, for he was to be killed. And so it proved to be, for he was never seen again. When the fog rolled away, Ohkinhedhe, looking down from the sky, perceived his son lying dead. With rage in his heart he sought the murderers, and meeting Nfimak-mahana accused him of the deed. The other, however, denied all knowledge of it, and then, being asked to bury the body, he carried it to a hilltop and with his staff split open a great black boulder. There, in the cleft he laid the body of the son of Ohkihedhe, and closed the rock, which still is marked with a line of red blood. ✿

Coyote Transforms Evil Creatures (*Kalispel*)

COYOTE MARRIED GOPHER, and they had four sons. As he was one day traveling about, he saw a lodge pitched close beside a small lake. He heard singing. He stopped and listened more closely, and then heard speaking, the voice telling how Coyote was coming down the hill. He wondered if they were speaking about him, and in order to decide if they were, he turned and walked up the hill, and truly enough, the song now changed and the words explained that Coyote was going up the hill. Then he went forward to the lodge, and inside he saw a crowd of women, handsome women with fine earrings. He entered and began to dance with them. After a while one of them seized him, then another, and then all crowded around him. They raised him from the ground, bore him out of the lodge, all the time dancing, and went toward the lake. Seeing that they intended to enter the water, Coyote begged that he be permitted to remove his clothing so that it would not be wet, but they answered, "Never mind your clothing, you will get better garments." Then they walked into the water, and in the deep water they held him until he was drowned. They let his body go. It floated to the surface, and drifted away to the other shore. Coyote's friend, Yellow Fox, found the body there, and to himself he said: "Here is Coyote, my friend. You must have been doing something to the Clams, and now you are dead." He stepped over the body, and it arose, alive once more. "I must have been asleep," said Coyote. But Yellow Fox was not to be deceived, and he said, "You must have been doing something to the Clams, and they killed you." "Yes, it is true," admitted

36. Oscar Makes Cry—Ponca

37. Noatak man

Coyote, "I will go back and destroy them." "You had better not go back," remonstrated his friend; "they may kill you again." Nevertheless Coyote returned and placed fire all around their lodge; then going to the hill above, he sat down to watch, and when the fire was well started, he called to the Clams: "There is a fire starting around your home; it will destroy every one of you! You are handsome women!" The Clams came running out, while Coyote sat and laughed at them, advising them to run to a dry place, which they in their ignorance did, but the fire still pursued them, and some of them were burned in the back. He laughed, and said: "Don't you know anything? Go toward the trees, where they have been barked, and rub your backs in the pitch, and the fire will go out." They did even that, knowing no better. "Go down into that slough, where it is dry and the grass is thick and long, and you will save yourselves," advised Coyote. They went into the slough, and all were burned. Then Coyote called out: "You do not know anything. You do not deserve to be a people. Go down to the water, and always live there!" So they went into the water and saved themselves from being completely consumed, and since that time they have been like the clams which we find in the water. Resuming his travels, Coyote encountered a lodge in which he found no people, but a great mass of utensils of every sort piled up inside. Thinking to take away as many rolls of tule matting as he could carry, he tried to open a roll, to see how large and good it was, but as soon as be started to handle it, the matting began to envelop him. Then the other rolls came and wrapped themselves closely around him, and soon he was dead, smothered by the Tule people. They cast his body outside. By and by came Yellow Fox, who saw his friend, paused, stepped over the body, and made it again alive. Coyote sat up, rubbed his eyes, and pretended that he had been sleeping; but his friend was not deceived, and said, "You had better not go back there, for you were killed by the Tules." Coyote, however, insisted on returning and destroying them by fire. Back he went and set fire all around their lodge, saying to them, "In the future you shall not have power to kill people; you shall be good only for covering lodges." Next Coyote came to a lodge which contained many beautiful women, two of whom he thought he would take for his wives. They began to brush his hair, and he lay down to enjoy the sensation, but the brushing became violent, and soon all the hair was scratched from his body, and he was thrown out of the lodge dead. Again he was restored by Yellow Fox, who told him he had been destroyed by the Brush people. Coyote went back to the lodge, and set fire around it; then as the people burned, he said: "You shall no longer be a people with power to kill others, but you shall be used only to brush hair, or to brush berries from the bushes." Many other evil creatures Coyote transformed into useful articles. ✽

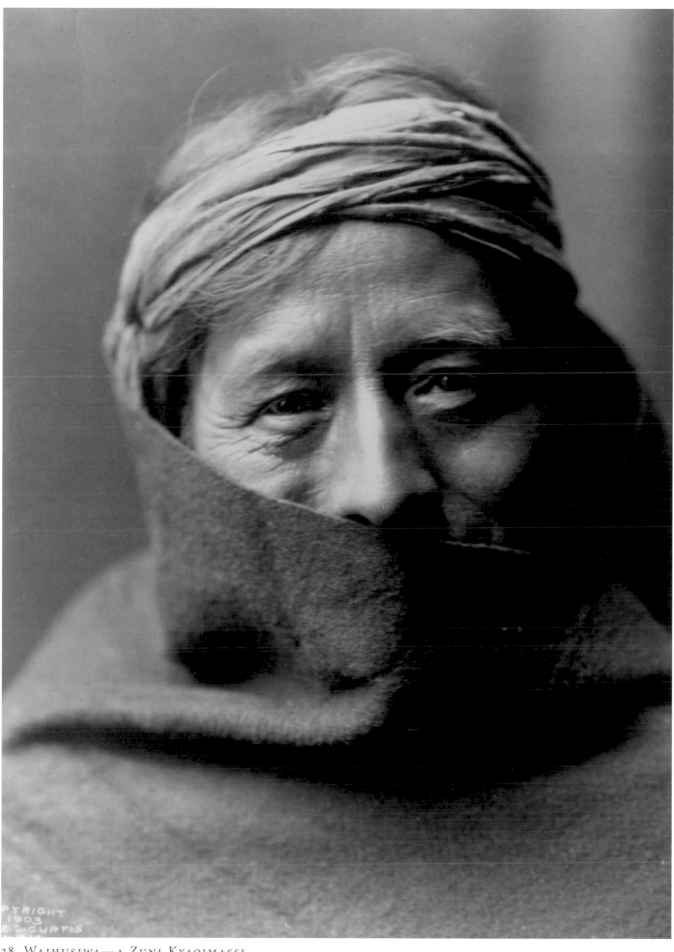

38. Waihusiwa—a Zuni Kyaqimassi

X1822-05

39. Coe Opa

40. Kihsuk—Selawik

41. TAHOPIK—DIOMEDE

Crawfish and Grizzly-bear Contend *(Sinkiuse)*

Crawfish considered himself a great fighter, and Grizzly-bear entertained the same opinion about himself. Coyote, a cunning trouble-maker, went to tell Grizzly-bear what he had heard Crawfish say; then he reported to Crawfish what he had heard the other tell about his own power. Said Crawfish, "If Grizzly-bear says that he is the greater, he had better come and fight." Then Coyote arranged that the two were to meet at a certain place and decide which was the stronger. When the fight began, Grizzly-bear tried to seize his opponent in his teeth, but the latter caught him by the lip and pulled until Grizzly-bear gave way and followed, howling with pain. Crawfish held on until the other promised to go home at once and cease his boasting, but as soon as he was loose Grizzly-bear tried again to bite, only to be caught again by the lip and dragged about. At last Grizzly-bear gave up and went home, but as he started away Crawfish caught hold of the hair under his belly and thus was carried along. When Grizzly-bear got home he sat down and said to himself, "I will not tell any one that Crawfish got the better of me." Crawfish reached out and pinched him by the neck, and demanded, "What was that you said?" "I did not say anything," protested Grizzly-bear. "I heard what you said," insisted the other; "I heard from where you left me and jumped all the way here!" Grizzly-bear was then convinced that Crawfish was the more powerful, and acknowledged it.

Coyote and Salmon *(Wishham)*

Chinook Salmon, who had four wives: Mouse, Goldfinch, Dove, and Cricket; was a great hunter, and spent much of his time in the pursuit of game. Dove had one child, but there were no other children. Coyote was living with this family, but it was his habit to spend his time roaming about the country. One day he failed to return. "Where is old man?" asked Salmon, but nobody knew. A little later, however, he came in. "Where have you been, grandfather?" asked Salmon. "Grandson," he replied, "my people used to trap eagles, and I have been looking for eagles. I saw two young ones in a nest." "Where did you see two eagles? We will go there to-morrow and get them," said Salmon. "It is not far from here," Coyote assured him. The next morning they started out toward the mouth of the river, and came to a high bluff, where they saw a nest in a tree which stood on the edge of the rock. They looked at it a while, and saw two eaglets open their wings, which made Salmon very anxious to get those fine feathers. He told Coyote to remain below while he climbed the tree. "Before you go," counseled Coyote, "take off your fine clothing, beads, and shells, and leave them here." "Why?" asked the other. "That is the way the old people used to get eagles," explained Coyote. So Salmon took off his finery and began to climb. Now Coyote started to make medicine that the tree might grow higher. Salmon heard him muttering words, and called down, "What are you saying?" "I say, you are getting close now," cried Coyote, "keep your eyes on the birds or they will fly away!" Salmon continued to climb, but the tree kept growing. At last, however, he reached the nest, only to find it empty. He looked down, and found himself so far above the ground that it made him dizzy; and more than that, he saw Coyote, dressed in the clothing and ornaments he had left below, traveling homeward. Coyote went back to their house, and took for his wives the

42. Les Ping, Captain Koya (or Kopi)—Buffalo Mountain

43. UNKNOWN—SELAWIK OR NUNIVAK WOMAN

two for whom Salmon had never seemed to care—Mouse and Goldfinch. He told them that the eagles had flown away, and that Salmon had gone to live with some friends and did not intend to come back to his wives, for he was tired of them. The next morning Coyote said that they would move their camp, and, though Dove and Cricket did not trust him, they decided to go along. They followed, and in the evening made a camp apart from the other three, for they would not be wives of Coyote. The next day the journey was continued, and it began to rain. This was the tears of Salmon, who in the meantime had climbed down the tree, but could not descend the face of the rock until he caused a stream of water, his tears, to flow over the cliff. He found his home deserted, but he followed the trail of his wives. Dove was carrying her baby, walking beside Cricket. Five days Salmon had been following, and now he came up behind the two women, who were weeping. When they saw their husband, they were overjoyed, and quickly gave him clothing. The three then followed the others, and after a while Coyote caught sight of Salmon. Immediately he began to cry, and to take off Salmon's clothing and ornaments, which he begged Salmon to take back, but the other refused them, saying: "You may keep them. You have spoiled them. You told me a lie and made me feel sad. If you had told me you wanted these two women, you could have had them." The six stopped and built two houses. The next morning Salmon went hunting, and later in the day returned with deer meat, some of which he gave to Coyote. "I have left a great deal of meat in the mountains," he said. "Tomorrow we can get it, and you may have it." So the next morning both started out for the mountains. They crossed a dry creek-bed at the foot of the mountains, and it began to rain. They went a little farther, and saw a great quantity of deer meat hanging in the trees. "Coyote," said Salmon, "you take all you can. Take it all; I do not need any." So Coyote loaded up with all he could possibly carry. Salmon said he would go on up the hill and kill another deer before returning, and Coyote started back alone. When he came to the first creek, he found a good deal of water running down, but he managed to cross. The second creek was deeper, the third still deeper, and the fourth nearly too deep to ford. It was still raining, and in the middle of the last watercourse he fell, the head-strap dropped down about his neck, and the load of meat pulled his head under water. He lost consciousness, and his body floated down the stream, finally lodging on some branches. He regained his senses, and, looking up and seeing the surface of the rushing water, thought it was clouds blown by the wind. He got up, but fell again, and once more was carried down by the current. At length he came to the Columbia River, and after a while his body caught on a stump. Here he again recovered consciousness, but try as he would, he could discover no land. He made use of his medicine-power, and said, "After a while there will be land here," and soon there was a small island. He sat there, and after he was rested he made a hut. There he was compelled to remain. One day he saw Swans flying overhead. The birds thought it strange that there should be an island where they had never seen one before, and flew lower to examine it. They saw a person sitting there. Their chief said, "If we find that this man is alone, we can go down and look at him." Then he continued: "If we find he is alone, we can take him home and our youngest sister can have him for a husband." They flew very low, saw that there was a single person there, and alighted. The eldest asked, "Are you alone?" "Yes," said Coyote. "Can we take you away with us?" Swan continued. "We have a sister, and you can marry her." "All right, all right! Take me along!" said Coyote eagerly. The

X1775-05

44. Ambrosio Martinez—San Juan

45. Selawik woman

46. A Cupeño woman (large)

two largest put their wings together, and Coyote sat on them, holding to their necks, and thus was borne away. They told him to shut his eyes, and not to open them until they got home. They flew far across the water to their home, and there Coyote married the Swan woman. These Swans hunted deer and carried them home on their wings across the water. Coyote proved a good husband, and an industrious provider of wood in the absence of the brothers. They felt very happy, for their sister had a husband, and there was always plenty of wood when they returned tired from the hunt. After a while Coyote wearied of gathering wood, and desired to hunt deer, and they agreed to take him. So the next morning they carried him across the water, where he found a land full of game of every kind. The next day he was again taken to the hunt. Thrice the Swans carried him across the water, and each time Coyote observed that they made a certain sound when they flew. "That is the way they are able to fly," he thought. "If I could make that sound, I too could fly." The fourth time they carried him, he tried and succeeded in making the right sound. They were near land, and the Swans thought that now their brother must be able to fly, since he had the voice of a Swan; so they opened their wings, when down Coyote tumbled into the water. He drifted down the river until he caught hold of some roots and crawled ashore. Once more he was a wanderer. ✤

Why Wolves Do Not Eat the Stomach of a Deer *(Clayoquot)*

When the animals were people, Deer and his little son were fishing, and the boy fell asleep. Some Wolf people passed in a canoe, and Deer derided them, speaking so low that they did not hear him. Another canoe passed, and again he said: "Are you going home, you raw-eaters?" They asked what he had said, and he answered, "I just spoke about your having such a fine day to move." But they had heard his insult, and they dragged him out of his canoe into theirs, leaving the little boy asleep in the canoe. So he became a slave to the chief of the Wolves. The wife of the chief one day ordered him to sharpen two knives for her. He went to the beach, and as he rubbed the shell knives on the stone, he sang: "Knife, knife, knife, knife, knife! I am making sharp a knife for the woman Wolf chief! Qitl, qitl, qitl, qitl!" He decided to hide one of the knives and say that it was broken; so he placed it at the corner of the house, and took the other to the Wolf woman, saying, "I broke one." She asked where he had thrown it, and he answered, "It was broken in small pieces that could not be put together, and I threw them into the water." That night the chief said to Deer, "Come and tell me a story that will make me sleep." So Deer sat beside him as he lay on the floor leaning his head against the bed, and began to tell a story; and soon the chief and all the others fell asleep. Then Deer slipped out and recovered the knife, cut off the chief's head and placed it on the prow of a canoe, and paddled for home, singing a boasting song about the Wolf chief's head. When the chief's wife awoke, she gave him a push and said, "Come to bed!" There was no response, and she perceived that the floor was wet. When she looked more closely and saw that his head was gone, she began to wail, and the people rushed in. It was soon discovered that Deer was missing. Living in that village was Aupuwaik ["wren"], who could see everything, no matter how far away. He saw where Deer was, and called on Crane to bring out his box and release a fog. So Crane opened his box, and fog covered the water so thickly that Deer could not see his way, and, becoming confused,

47. Unknown—Piegan or Arapaho man

48. QUNANINRU—KING ISLAND

49. A CHUKCHANSI WOMAN

X1656-05

50. Pah Toi (White Clay)

returned to the Wolf village, thinking he was on his way home. Now the Wolves, with teeth sharpened in anticipation, were waiting on the beach. Deer stepped ashore, and then saw the Wolves. He leaped into a tree, and the Wolves, unable to follow him, began to gnaw off the roots; but when the tree fell, Deer leaped into another. So it went, until the Wolves, exhausted, assembled to discuss what they should do. Nobody knew what was best, and they sent for Wren. As he came in, Elk sneered, "Such a little man, and we always have to wait for him!" Wren sat down beside him and said: "Well, why do not you think, and make up your mind about this, you big man? Such a big nosed thing!" "I will crush you with my arm if you do not keep silence," threatened Elk. "Try it, and I will go into your nose!" answered Wren. But Elk would not give up the quarrel, and suddenly Wren darted into his nostril, and the big man began to sneeze. When he was almost dead, Wren came out, and they were at peace with each other. Then Wren taught them a song about the arms and legs of Deer falling down from the tree, and they were to sing it while dancing around the tree. Lying there was a fallen tree with one end raised above the ground, and in passing under it they forgot the song and had to go back to Wren. Four times this happened before they knew the song, and then they sang it four times, going about the tree four times. One of Deer's legs fell down, and the Wolves leaped upon it and devoured it. Thus successively were brought down and devoured the other leg, the two arms, and the body of Deer. But the stomach was not eaten, for Deer had begged them not to eat it. That is why wolves never eat the stomach of a deer. ✿

Coyotes Fail to Catch the Young Crows (*Hopi*)

I-tuwufsi! As Is-mo-wala "coyote mouth gap" — a place south of Oraibi, so called from a fancied resemblance to the mouth of a coyote] Coyote was living. One day he went rabbit hunting down the valley to Siu-tsomo ["onion knoll"], and while wandering along he came upon a nest of crows among the rocks. He could not quite reach them, so he started home for help, and on the way he killed a rabbit. The next morning he boiled the rabbit, and going out a little way from his home, he howled and barked toward the north. Soon there came a Coyote running at full speed. He dashed up, made a sharp turn, and stopped. "What is it?" he asked.

"While I was hunting rabbits," said the other, "I found a nest of young crows, and I want you to help me get them." "Ali ['good eating']!" said the newcomer. Coyote then repeated his howling and barking toward the west, and another Coyote came running from that direction. Thus also he brought a Coyote from the south, and another from the east. After he had explained his purpose to the last arrival, they ate the rabbit and set out for the crows' nest.

Having reached the place they began to ponder how they should get at the crows. They decided to suspend themselves downward from the upper edge of the rock, one holding the other, and the smallest going first. It was determined also that they should keep their eyes closed, so as to avoid dizziness. The smallest was lowered over the edge by the next larger, who held his tail in his mouth. Then the next larger took hold of the tail of the second one, and so it went. But when the largest was holding the weight of the other edge by the next larger, who held his tail in his mouth. Then the next larger took hold of the tail of the second one, and so it went. But when the largest

51. Paviotso—female type

X1803-05

52. OHIN TSAU—SANTA CLARA

53. TEJON SERRANO—KITANEMUK

was holding the weight of the other four suspended below him, still the first could not quite reach the crows. He called to the one at the top of the rock to come a little closer to the edge. At this point the Coyote in the middle of the line opened his eyes to see how far the first one was from the nest. The two below him were straining so hard to bridge the intervening distance that the anus of each was stretched wide, and excrement was being squeezed out. At this sight he laughed aloud, and the two below him plunged to the bottom. The fourth Coyote opened his eyes to see what was the matter, and observing the one below him in the same condition that had caused so much merriment, he too bust out laughing and let the one below him fall. The one on the edge of the cliff now opened his eyes and began to laugh at the same sight, and thus the fourth fell, while the last one laughed so heartily that he fell off the cliff and perished with the other four. Paiyasava! ✿

Prairie-falcon, Chicken-hawk, and the Monster (*Yokuts*)

PRAIRIE-FALCON [Limik] and Chicken-hawk [Pohyun] went up the river. Prairie-falcon saw a red salmon. He pointed it out to his brother, and said, "Do you see that salmon?" For a long time Chicken-hawk could not see it. Then when he saw it he threw a stone at it. The salmon did not move. He threw a stick, and the salmon swallowed it. He took an arrow and said, "I would like to see him swallow this." He threw it, and the salmon swallowed it. He drew out of his fox-skin quiver all his arrows and threw them at the salmon, which swallowed them all. He threw in his brother's arrows, and they were swallowed. He threw both bows, and they were swallowed. Then he said, "Well, I would like to see if he can swallow me!" He leaped in, and was swallowed. Prairie-falcon stood there a long time, thinking what to do. "Well," he said, "I too might as well die." He jumped in and the salmon swallowed him. It did not move from that place. Prairie-falcon felt something round. He asked, "What is this?" Chicken-hawk felt of it and said: "It is his heart. I think he would die if we cut it off." Prairie-falcon had a small knife tied about his neck. He gave it to his brother, who cut off the heart. He said: "It will go north. Hold on!" The salmon went northward to the ocean, and from there it went southward to the ocean, and then westward to the ocean. Then it came to the river [San Joaquin] and threw itself out on the sand. It lay there gasping, and Prairie-falcon, peering out through its opening and closing mouth, saw the sand. He said: "What is that? Is it water or land? Well, I am going out to see what it is, even if I die." He took the white sperm and rubbed it between the palms of his hands until it was like down. He gave it to his brother. When the salmon's mouth opened again, he leaped forward, and his brother blew on the dry substance and blew him out. He landed on the dry sand, and laughed with joy. He called to his brother that it was good, and Chicken-hawk jumped out. "This salmon is good to eat," said Prairie-falcon. He showed his brother how to cut it into strips. "Build a fire and dry it, and then cook it, and if you wish to eat it, do so. I am going to sleep." Chicken-hawk cut the salmon up and put the strips before the fire. They smelled good. He ate some. They were good. He cooked more and ate. Suddenly while he was hanging up some strips there was a great sound, as if something were gulping food. He looked, and saw that the meat he was cooking had disappeared. He did not know what was the cause. He was angry. He said, "I will cook more." He took his arrows from the salmon's stomach and sat with them

STORIES AND FACES

115

54. Cheyenne matron

55. BLACK BEAR—CHEYENNE

behind his back, waiting to see what had taken his food. Something came out of the ocean and reached for the food. He shot an arrow and struck it in the eye before it could get back into the water. Its mother began to sing, "You have shot my baby in the eye!" It was this Shanwiwa that had put Prairie-falcon to sleep by magic. Chicken-hawk could hear her coming, and was frightened. He shook his brother and tried to waken him. He took a glowing stick and burned him beside the ear, and thus woke him. When Prairie-falcon saw what had happened, he said: "Why did you kill this? Well, we had better go north now. We must leave this place." So they ran away, and Shanwawa pursued them over the land, sucking in her breath with a terrible noise. That was the way she secured her prey. Her breath threatened to draw them back into her mouth. At last they came to their aunt Stink-bug [Badedut]. But they ran on. When Shanwawa came to this place, she demanded to know where they were. "Oh, they are here," said Stink-bug. "But you are tired. Rest a while, and then I will give them to you." When Shanwawa had rested, Stink-bug said, "Shut your eyes and open your mouth, and I will throw them into it." Shanwawa did so, and Stink-bug threw into her throat a great quantity of that which she made for stinks. Shanwawa rolled over and over in a dizzy convulsion. But when she recovered, she ran on. In succession the brothers passed their other relations, Red Ant, Small Skunk, and Great Skunk. Lastly they came to their aunt Timlaichi [a bug]. When Shanwawa arrived there, Timlaichi made her rest a while, and then threw into her mouth a red-hot stone, which burned its way completely through her body and killed her. ✿

Coyote and Talkakuna *(Yokuts)*

TALKAKUNI LIVED AT CHUKCHANO [north of Apaso, Fresno flat]. At that place he cooked the people whom he captured as they gathered pine-nuts in the hills. When he saw anyone in a tree he would throw a large round stone and kill him. Thus he had killed nearly all the people, and Coyote determined to stop him. He went hunting jack-rabbits and cooked them, and took the meat with him so that he would not have to eat human flesh. He made himself look like an old woman. At Chukchano he found only the two children of Talkakuna. They offered him meat, but he refused it, saying he would wait until evening, because he was not hungry. When Talkakuna was heard coming, the children ran to Coyote and said, "Our grandfather is here!" Then Talkakuna entered. He said: "We will eat soon. There is plenty of meat." Coyote had made a small hole in the ground, in which he concealed the human flesh that was given to him, while he secretly ate his rabbit meat. Then he asked Talkakuna to sing, and he listened, with hands crossed on his knees and one foot keeping time. He asked the children to have their grandfather remove his moccasins and rest his feet, and while Talkakuna sang and the children listened, he hid them, so that the next morning Talkkuna had to go hunting barefoot. During the day while the children were swimming Coyote built a large fire. He told them to go close to it and warm themselves, then suddenly he pushed them in and killed them. Next he covered the ground with thorns. In the evening Talkakuna came and whistled for his children. He heard what seemed to be their answer. Then Coyote shouted, and Talkakuna knew that his grandchildren had been killed. He rushed up, but trod on the thorns, and one of them pierced his heart, which was in his foot. And so he died. ✿

56. Jack Rowan—Chukchansi Yokut

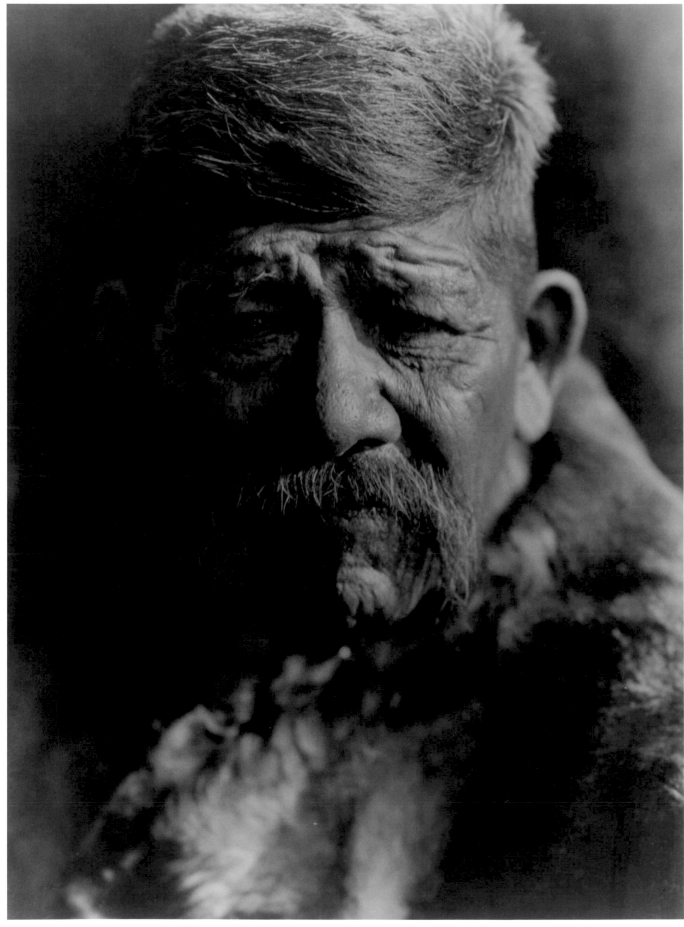

57. A chief—Chukchansi Yokut

58. UNKNOWN—SERRANO, DIEGUEÑO, OR CUPEÑO WOMAN

59. OLD "UKIAH"—POMO

Coyote Steals the Morning-star *(Yokuts)*

THERE WAS NO SUN. It was dark. But far in the east Coyote could hear birds sing when their morning came. So he went to see what was there. The people were hunting rabbits. As they went homeward after the hunt, a great tree fell across the trail. This was Coyote. They tried to lift it, but there was only one man strong enough to do so, and he carried it home. He laid it near the morning star and tried to make a fire, but it would not burn. So Coyote, in the form of a log, lay there a long time watching the morning star, observing how Turtle kept gradually rising and revealing it more and more, and daylight approached. At last Coyote seized the star and ran, and the people pursued him in vain. When he brought the star home, he tried it in various places; but only in the east would it shine brightly, so there he left it. ✿

Antelope Races with Hawk *(Nambe/San Juan/San Ildefonso)*

AT PERAGE LIVED AN OLD WOMAN WITH HER GRANDSON, a little boy. One day he asked her to make a bow, arrows, and bread, for he intended to hunt deer. The old woman wept: "What can you do? You are only a child. Something will eat you." "Well, grandmother," he said, "I will try. We are poor; we have little food. I must do what I can." So she made what he wished, and the next morning he set out with the prayer-sticks she had prepared for him. He soon reached the forested mountains, and at once planted the sticks. In the afternoon he found a herd of deer, which came running toward him. They came close, and a buck stopped, threw up its head, and gazed at him. His bow twanged, and the animal fell dead. He flayed it with his obsidian knife, cut off as much meat as he could carry, and packed it home. His grandmother rejoiced. The next day he killed a turkey, the third day some rabbits. On the fourth morning, not far from the village, he saw two men coming up behind him. He sat down on a stone to wait. "Where are you going?" they asked. He told them he was hunting, and they asked if he wished to race. He agreed, and they said that he might have four days in which to prepare. He inquired who would run for them, and they told him it would be Hawk. "I will have Antelope," he decided. "Good! If you win, we will become snakes, and if we win we will kill you!" "Good!" said the boy, and turned homeward to inform his grandmother what had occurred. "My little boy," she cried, "what shall we do now? You are only a child, and what can you do?" "Anyway, I am going to race, for I have promised." He told her to make prayer-sticks and give smoke and meal to them, so that he could make offerings. The next day he took the prayer-sticks and meal and prayed to the Antelope, and gave them the offerings. The next day he went forth again. Butterfly fluttered up to him and said: "I see that you are sad, that you are in trouble. I will help you. Follow me; I will take you to my house." Among the hills they came to a large rock and a trickling spring. She told him to enter. "How can I get in?" he asked. "Why, walk right in." "But there is no door," he said. Butterfly opened a doorway right through the solid rock and the boy went in. She told him to sit down, and then asked what was going on in his village. When he explained the wager he had made, she assured him that he need not fear. "Go home," she said, "and tomorrow come to the place where I met you today." The boy went home comforted. The next morning he

60. SANTO DOMINGO MAN

X1751-05

61. Tse-ka—Cacique of San Juan

returned to the meeting-place and was led again to Butterfly's house. She left him waiting there, but soon returned with Antelope Boy. "Here is Antelope Boy," she said. "Take him home, but let no one see him until tomorrow." At home he concealed Antelope Boy in a back room, and while he ate, the two men came to inquire if he were ready for the next day's race. He asked what time they would begin, and they said, "We will start in the morning immediately after breakfast." His grandmother was praying to all the Okuwa [cloud-gods] for help. The next morning the men returned and proposed that they run four times around the mountain south of San Ildefonso. So it was agreed, and the race began. Hawk was very swift, and gained steadily. But on the second round clouds began to appear, and during the third circuit a heavy rain fell. Soon Hawk's feathers were so wet that he was unable to fly, and Antelope Boy passed him and won the race. The two men immediately became the first snakes. ✾

Destruction of Sikyatki *(Hopi)*

I-TUWUFSI! There were people living at Kuchaptuvela and at Sikyatki, and for some time there had been bad feeling between the two villages. Two young men of Sikyatki went to the other pueblo, and while a maiden was parching meal they shot her in the side. The arrow passed through the body and killed her, and the meal, untended, burned, and smoke filled the room. The parents of the girl in the room below smelled the smoke, and the mother went up to see what was the matter. Thus they discovered her body. The brother of the murdered girl was very angry, and having planned his revenge began secretly to practice running at night. Winter passed and spring came, and he began to go to Sikyatki occasionally to ascertain if there would be a Kachina dance soon. After a time he learned that there would be an evening dance of the Katsinamu. The next day he secured a mask, and painted it to represent Homson-Katsina, and in the afternoon he took his mask and went along the side of the cliff on the west side of the mesa, so that nobody at Sikyatki might see him. At a point opposite Sikyatki he waited until late in the afternoon, and when the Katsinamu started dancing, he crossed the mesa, went down into the village, and entered the plaza from the south side while the dancers were performing. With his mask on he ran about the plaza for a time, personating Homson-Katsina and when he caught a youth he would cut off a small lock of hair and put it under his sash. Then looking up at the spectators on the housetops, he singled out the chief's daughter, and ran up to the roof. All the girls fled into the houses, and he followed the chief's daughter. The girls who had taken refuge in that house were huddled together in one corner. He leaped among them and dragged out the chief's daughter, and cut off her head. Back to the house-top he dashed, brandishing the head so that everybody could see it, and then leaped to the ground and fled, with the young men of Sikyatki in pursuit. The avenger ran along the cliff on the east side of the mesa, and when the pursuers were at Monwi-va ["chief spring"], he was already at Wala ["gap"]. So they gave up the chase and returned to Sikyatki. When the young man got back home with the head, he went into the kiva, where the old men were smoking. He placed it beside the fireplace, removed his mask, and said: "Now I have carried out my plan. I have been getting ready for this through all kinds of weather. I have been enduring the hardship of cold weather, and

62. UNKNOWN

63. CHARLIE WOOD—KOBUK

64. Su-donii (Osier-Willow Blossom)—Pyramid Lake Paviotso

65. Why Wn Se Wa

running about the country while you have been sound asleep. Just to do this I have been practicing running. Now I have fulfilled my plan. I am relieved." When he had removed all of his Kachina costume, he took the head out and buried it. The people of Sikyatki, and especially the chief, mourned greatly, and about planting time he one day went to Kuchaptuvela. The chief of this village inquired, "Why have you come?" "I have been wondering about our lives. There has been trouble between us, and I do not want either village to stand. My village will be the first one to be destroyed. After that the people of your village may do as they please regarding the destruction of this place. You will be notified when to come." This matter was a secret between the two chiefs, and soon after this it was announced at Sikyatki that the people were to plant corn for the chief. On the day of the announcement the chief went again to Kuchaptuvela and reported that on the fourth day following his people would go forth to plant corn for him. He directed that the warriors of Kuchaptuvela should enter Sikyatki after the people had gone down into the valley, when only women and children would be left in the houses. The signal would be given by the chief's wife, who would appear on the roof of her house and throw out some refuse. At this instant the warriors were to rush down into the village from the top of the mesa. She was then to wash her head, and while she was doing this they were to behead her, and then treat the others likewise. These were the instructions given by the chief of Sikyatki. His wife was in the secret, but none other among the people of Sikyatki knew it. On the morning of the appointed day the warriors set out from Kuchaptuvela, and on the top of the mesa above Sikyatki, they waited, watching the people descend into the cornfields. Soon the chief's wife appeared on the housetop and threw out a basket of refuse. This dirt represented her people, whom she was consigning to destruction. Then they rushed down straight to the chief's house and cut off the woman's head while she was in the act of washing her hair, after which they proceeded among the houses and killed all the women and children. They set fire to the woodwork of the houses, and when the people below in the fields saw the smoke, they hurried back and met the warriors at the foot of the mesa. But having no weapons they were easily killed. Only a few escaped, and these went to Oraibi and to Kuchaptuvela. Paiyasava ["this how long"]! ✸

The Girl Who Married Grizzly-bear and Acquired the Dance Tlu'wulahu (*Bellabella*)

Tlaqagiluyoqa ["born to be copper-maker woman"], the daughter of a chief of high rank, was so proud that she was unwilling to marry; she refused every suitor. Her wrists and ankles were covered with rings of copper. One day she ordered her two female slaves to accompany her to a berry-patch, and as they gathered the fruit the girl stepped on the droppings of a grizzly-bear. "Oh," she exclaimed, "that dirty creature comes to walk in this place and leaves that filth for me to step on and soil my feet!" "Do not say so!" cautioned the women. "The spirit of the creature which dropped that is with us all the time." But the girl did not cease to upbraid the bear. They filled their baskets, covered the berries with skunk-cabbage leaves, and laced the tops shut. Then they swung the baskets on their backs and started homeward. Soon the handle of the girl's basket, which had been perfectly sound, broke, and the berries were spilled. She called the slaves, who gathered up the fruit, repaired

66. Unknown

67. JIMMIE MAJOR WAILAIKI, SEGEL GENTLE (ALMOST KILLED)

68. KOSHONONO—POMO

the handle, and placed the basket again on her back. But it broke again, and this time the slaves did not hear her call and walked right on. The girl stopped and picked up the scattered berries, and just before she was ready to raise the basket to her back, she saw two men. One of them, a very handsome youth, said, "Let me carry your berries." Without inquiring who they were, she gave him the basket and they walked along the trail toward the village. They stepped over a log, and the woman felt changed in some subtle manner. Again a step was taken over another log, and again she experienced the strange feeling. Thus they stepped over four logs, and then she saw ahead a great village, and heard the people cry out, " Here comes our chief with his wife!" Then she realized that she had been stolen by this man. He led her into a very large house, and he seemed to change. He became rough, instead of kind and gentle, and his voice was very harsh. The two men left her there and passed outside. Apparently she was alone. But some one in the corner spoke: "Come hither. I am Tlopakyahtulihl ['rooted to the floor'], and since I cannot move, you must come to me." The girl went to that corner and found a very old woman, who said: "You are the woman that stepped on the Grizzly-bear's droppings, and you said some bad words against that Grizzly-bear. The man who left those droppings is the very one who brought you here, and your life is depending on what you do when you first go to the beach to defecate. The best thing is to go now and practice what you will do. Fear not. Whenever you go to the beach, dig a hole secretly, and if you wish to defecate, you may do so in that hole. But be careful to cover it well, and then take one of your copper rings and leave it there: they will think that was what you dropped. You had better go now, and you will see what they will say to you. The Grizzly-bears are all away fishing, except one who is watching constantly." The girl decided to try it at once, and went to the beach. Immediately the watchman called, and the Grizzly-bears came hurrying back. After digging the hole she sat there for a while, then filled it with sand, and on the top laid one of her copper bracelets. As soon as she got up, the people came, and with a small stick a man lifted the bracelet and looked at it. "It is little wonder she talked so proudly!" he exclaimed. "Her excrement is copper!" And they began to play with the ring, tossing it to one another. Tlaqagiluyoqa went into the house, and the old woman asked, "Did you do it right?" "Yes, I am here alive." "Whenever you become homesick, tell me. Here is one thing you must know: they are going to put two little children to be with you constantly. Whenever your husband goes fishing, you will have to collect firewood. Go to the woods for it, not to the beach. Every day go farther and farther from the house, and always be careful to put the fuel on the backs of the children. Make them lean up against a tree when you put the bundle on their backs. All the women go to the beach for wood, and gather the small sticks that lie on the bottom in the water." So the young woman started out for wood with the two children, whom she loaded with fagots. She piled fuel on the fire, awaiting the return of her husband, and the Grizzly-bear women kindled their fires. But their water soaked wood made a great deal of steam, while hers burned freely. Then her husband came in, his bear-skin all wet. He threw it off and shook it over the fire, and the blaze was extinguished. Then he beat the girl with the skin. The other Grizzly-bears, coming into their houses, removed their wet skins and shook them over the fires, and the steaming sticks blazed. Day by day the girl's copper rings became fewer. One day her downheartedness was plainly evident on her face and in her demeanor, and the old woman said, "You wish to go home." "Yes," admitted the girl.

69. A Cupeño woman

X1880-06

70. THE APACHE

"Well, tomorrow morning get a stick from a salmonberry bush and bring it to me." The next morning she went into the woods for fuel, and after walking a long distance, she broke off a piece of salmonberry bush and carried it while the children bore the fagots. When the old woman received the stick she measured from it the length of her forearm from elbow to knuckles. Then at equidistant points she gnawed off the bark in four places, and she said: "I think tomorrow you had better run away. Drop this stick to the ground, and it will point the way to your home." She gave the girl also a cedar stick, a stone, a tube of bladder-kelp containing oil, and a comb, and told her how to use them. "But one thing you must remember," she cautioned. "Tie those two children to trees. When you are putting the bundles on their backs, tie them to the trees so that they cannot escape." Early in the morning Tlaqagiluyoqa set out with the Grizzly-bear children. Having gathered her fagots she made the children lean back against a tree, as usual, and while tying the packs she wound the rope around the tree and bound them securely. Then she dropped the stick and ran in the direction it indicated. She heard the little Grizzly-bears scream, and she saw a great mountain right ahead. But she remembered no mountains on the road by which she had come, so she dropped the stick again. It fell straight toward the mountain. Then she remembered having stepped over four logs, and knew that in reality they had been mountains. Up the steep she ran, but behind was the growling of her pursuers. She passed the summit, and descended, but soon came to another height. By this time the Grizzly-bears were close, and she threw the comb over her shoulder. It became a tangled brake of thorny bushes, which delayed them. One after another the girl threw behind her the stone, the oil, and the cedar stick, and they became respectively a great mountain, a broad lake, and a tremendous tree that moved from side to side in the path of her pursuers. At length she reached salt water and saw a canoe containing a young man who wore a hat. He did not look around, and she called, "Come and take me in, and you shall have all my father's slaves for doing it!" The man tapped the gunwale with his paddle and it rang, and the canoe moved away from her. She called then, "Come ashore, and you shall have my father's name!" He tapped the gunwale again, and the canoe went out still farther. "Come ashore," she cried anxiously, "and take me in! You shall have everything my father possesses — his slaves, his dances, all!" He struck the canoe, and off it went still farther. Now she saw the Grizzly-bears coming, and in despair she begged him: "Come ashore and take me, and I will have you for my husband!" Then he struck the canoe, and immediately it came up beside her. She saw that his head was all copper, and so were the canoe and the paddle. She got in, he tapped the gunwale, and the craft shot out a little distance. In the bow was a spear, the two points of which kept thrusting themselves in and out, like the tongue of a serpent. Now the Grizzly-bears, clad in their shaggy skins, rushed angrily to the edge of the water, and the chief roared gruffly, "Bring my wife ashore, or we will kill you both!" The man in the canoe simply sat there without moving or speaking, and the girl perceived that he was handsome. To all the threats of the Grizzly-bears he made no response. Finally they plunged in and swam toward the canoe. Then the man spoke: "Spear, jump overboard and kill them!" That spear was a sisiutl. It leaped overboard, swam through the water, and darted through the bodies of the Grizzly-bears, one after another. Then it returned and lay down in the bow. Now the man addressed her: "Wife, be careful! You are in danger, just as with the people I have killed. I will not harm you, but it is my wife

71. Agoya Tsa (Star White)—Santa Clara

72. MONKEY FACE—MESA GRANDE DIEGUEÑO

73. A Pyramid Lake Paviotso

74. A Yauelmani Yokut

who will try to destroy you. When she eats, do not attempt to observe her. If you are behind her, she can see you just as if you were before her. Now we will go to yonder island, and I will kill those seals for her food." He tapped the canoe, and it darted to the island, where the sisiutl slipped out of the canoe and killed the seals. After piling them in the canoe he told Tlaqagiluyoqa to cover her head, and she did so. Then she heard him tap the gunwale and felt the copper canoe dart downward instead of forward. All the time her love for this man was growing, for he always spoke very kindly. Before long she felt the canoe ground on a beach, and heard the man get out in the water. He wrapped her up until she seemed to be only a roll of mats, took her under his arm, carried her into the house, and set her down in a corner. She heard people calling: "The canoe is full of seals! We will go and carry them up." Soon she heard them throwing the seals down from the doorway, and their bodies rolling down the steps; for the floor of this house was ten steps below the bottom of the sea, and it was called Tsuyakuq ["ten steps down "]. The wife of the man was crying hap! hap! hap! and Tlaqagiluyoqa heard her grasp the seals and devour them with a great crunching of bones. Every time a seal came rolling down, she uttered her hoarse cry and devoured it. The next morning the man carried out the roll of mats with the girl inside, and quickly the canoe rose to surface of the sea. There he removed the wrappings, and they began to converse. After a while she asked, "Why can I not see your other wife?" "She has something which she would throw at you," he answered, "and it would kill you. So you must not behold her." Then she asked, "Who are you? Who are you that are so kind to me?" "I am Komuqi, and my other name is Tlaqagila ['copper maker']. I know that your name is Tlaqagiluyoqa." Again he got his load of seals, and on their return placed her in a corner. So things went for a long time. In the company of her husband the girl was content; but in her gloomy corner, with her ears filled by the sound of the old woman devouring seals, she was very unhappy. She determined to see what the other woman was like, and one day when the seals were tumbling down the steps and the old woman was uttering her cries, Tlaqagiluyoqa pulled the mats down at the top and looked out. She saw only the back of a great fat creature holding a seal to her mouth. Instantly the seal eater cried "o!" and threw her hand back over her shoulder; and the young woman fell dead. Aware of all that was happening, Komuqi hurried in and demanded to know what she had done. "You have a stranger in this house," she said. He seized a spear and thrust it repeatedly into her body, but she only laughed. He tried to club her to death, but could not hurt her. Then he pondered how he might kill her, and the next day he made love to her and caressed her. "Where is your heart?" he asked. She laughed, and raised her foot, and showed him where it throbbed. "I do not believe it," he said, "My heart is in my breast. I will not believe yours is in your foot until I cut it out and see it." "Well," she said, "you can cut the foot open, but do not pull the heart out and cut it off." "No, I will only look at it," he promised, "and put the flesh back." He began to cut, but she experienced no pain. He cut deeper and saw the heart, a very small thing. "Do not touch it!" she exclaimed. "I must pull it out a little to see it. It does not look like my heart." He pulled it out, and quickly slashed it off, and she dropped lifeless. Komuqi unrolled the mats, in which was his young wife with blood running down from her mouth. He touched the heart to the mat beside her breast, first on one side then on the other, passing the heart four times directly over her chest. Then she sat up, rubbed her eyes, and said, "I have been sleeping long!" "Yes," he replied, "you have been sleeping soundly. Look at my big wife. I have killed her! This is her heart. I took it out of her, because she killed you." These two lived happily together, and the woman forgot her own people. After a period of only four months a boy was born, and Komuqi washed him in a copper dish. He seemed to handle the infant rather roughly. He made the child stand on the floor, while he held it and stepped on its toes. He pulled it upward by the arms, and it grew visibly. "That is large enough for one day," he said, and permitted her to wrap the child in sea-otter skin. On each of the three succeeding days he bathed and stretched the boy, and at the end of that time his son had become a young man and was given the name Tlaqagila. One day the young woman became lonesome and downhearted, and her husband, perceiving that she wished to see her parents, told her to make four eel-grass baskets small enough to fit over the end of the little finger. When these were ready he put a bit of copper in one of them, pieces of valuable skins in another, a splinter of his copper house in the third, and some of his food in the fourth. "All these you will take in the canoe," he announced. "Our son will accompany you. I will remain, yet I will be with you always. Now I am going to show you how I look." He turned himself into the huge, angry sea-monster, Komuqi. The monster disappeared, and again the man stood before her. "Do you want to carry that with you?" he asked. "Yes," she answered. "When there is dancing, that will belong to my son and to no one else." "I have a slave," he said, "and I will give you some dances." He summoned a strong man and commanded, "Take your place!" The slave lay down and became a Killer whale. "You will take this too," said Komuqi. The Killer whale suddenly disappeared, and the strong man stood there. Then the chief called another servant, a man with a great belly, who lay down and became Ku'ma [a fish with spines on the head, a large belly, and small body]. Next was called a man with a long neck, who, the chief said, was the watchman of the place. This man showed himself as Loon. Next the chief took a bit of something which his wife and son could not see, and put it into the small basket containing the copper broken from the house. He showed his son how to manage the canoe by tapping the gunwale, and warned his wife to cover herself while going up through the water. The four tiny baskets were placed in the canoe, and the woman in the bow covered herself; then her son in the stern tapped the gunwale. The canoe rose to the surface of the sea. The woman pointed and said: "That is your grandfather's house, the one with the great post before it. There is a stream at the left of the village: land among the salmonberry bushes." It was late evening, but not dark. The youth tapped the canoe, and at once it was among the bushes; and as soon as they stepped out, it vanished. At the same time the tiny baskets became enormous. Leaving them they went through the village and into the chief's house, the mother following her son. Everybody recognized her, for she had not changed. New mats were spread in the place of honor, and the villagers flocked in to see the woman and her son. When they were fed, the people watched to see if she would eat the food, wondering if her nature had been changed. She ate, but the young man did not; for in his mouth he constantly kept a small lump placed there by his father, so that he would never need other food. Then the woman told her father to send boys for the baskets; but the servants, unable to lift them, returned empty-handed. The youth Tlaqagila therefore transformed them into very small objects and carried them to the house in the palm of one hand. Three he placed in different corners of the room, but the fourth he said he would keep until everybody slept. He ordered that all retire early, even his mother, and late in the

75. Princess Angeline—daughter of Chief Seattle

76. A SOUTHERN MIWOK WOMAN

77. A Serrano (Kitanemuk) woman of Tejon

78. Pavaish—Pyramid Lake Paviotso

night he placed this fourth small basket, which contained the piece of copper broken from the house of his father, between the door and the fire. In the night the house of Komuqi came rising up out of the basket and took the place of the house in which it was set. As the roof rose, it lifted the roof of the wooden house, and the expanding walls crowded the wooden walls out. It also was "ten steps down." The small object which Komuqi had deposited in this basket without permitting either his wife or his son to see it was the mask of Komuqi. In front of the bedrooms of this copper house was a painted ma'wihl, and behind it the mask retired. From the first basket issued many coppers; from the second, robes of the skins of sea-otters and other animals of the sea; from the third, dry flesh of the whale and the hair-seal. Tlaqagila laid a piece of whale-meat on the beach, and it became four great, stranded whales. Then he lay down to sleep. Just at dawn there came from behind the mawihl the sound of wooden trumpets. All the people were awakened, and stood about in great astonishment. Even the chief's daughter had never heard this sound: but the spirit of Komuqi was within her and told her always what to do. She ordered her father to invite the people, and when all were assembled they heard voices singing behind the mawihl. The young man Tlaqagila came out wearing a small mask. He danced four songs with it, retiring after each song. Then appeared the great mask of the Komuqi, which danced once and retired. The spirit of Komuqi was dancing with it. Then the young man's mother danced four songs with the same small mask, and the spirit of killer whale danced four songs with the killer whale mask. All the singing was done by the spirits behind the mawihl. Then the chief himself danced with the small mask, and Ku'ma showed his own mask. The chief gave away the coppers, the robes, and the meat, and told the people to cut up the four whales on the beach. This was the origin of the first coppers and of the dance tlu'wulahu. ✸

The Woman Who Married a Horse *(Comanche)*

ONCE THERE WAS A WOMAN who became lost from the camp, and although they searched everywhere, they could not find her. It happened that two years later they returned to this camp-site and there found a number of wild horses grazing. As the horses ran off, they saw the woman running behind them. Some of the band mounted on their fastest horses and gave chase, surrounding the wild herd and roping the woman, whom they took back to camp. Because she was as wild as a horse, she fought so hard that her people had to tie her. In the course of time she became normal again and lived peaceably with her family. She had married a horse. ✸

Origin of Pine-nuts and Death *(Paviotso)*

COYOTE SMELLED PINE-NUTS IN THE EAST, and blood gushed from his nose. He traveled all day toward the odor; but he did not find the place, and returned. The next day he tried again, and discovered a place where there were many people. The chief was directing them to make the pine-nut mush very thin, for he did not want Coyote to carry it away. The children were holding mush tightly grasped in their little hands, and Coyote made them drop it by thumping their hands. But when he attempted to hold it in his mouth in order to carry it back to his people, it was so thin that he swallowed it. Then he went home again. His brother Wolf was making a speech to the assembled animal people, and Coyote stood beside him. Then all started out to obtain the pine-nuts, leaving behind only Sanaki [a small bird] to watch for their return. On the way they teased one another. Wildcat scratched the others, and when they complained, he showed his hands and rubbed them together to prove that he had no claws. The pine-nuts were concealed in the wrapping of a bow. All night they searched, and it was near morning when Louse found them and Woodpecker picked them out. Then they all ran westward, and the pine-nut people pursued them. Coyote said, "Let me be killed first." But Wolf said, "No, I will be the one." So he remained behind and was killed. Blackbird had on his leg a sore, in which they hid the nuts so that the pursuers would not be able to find them. When the people overtook them and searched in vain for the nuts, they killed all except Blackbird, who, pretending to be dead, flew onward after they had gone. When he arrived home, Sanaki helped him build a fire to parch the nuts. The eastern people made a great wall of ice between the dead western people and their home; but after a while Wolf came to life and revived his people, who broke through the ice wall and returned home. Wolf wanted the nuts to be like acorns, but Coyote said they should be in cones. And so it was. They discussed how many months should be in the year. Coyote placed his hands beside his forehead and said, "Perhaps there will be this many." Nobody replied. They sent him to another house for tobacco, and while he was absent they arranged that there should be three months in the summer, three in the winter, three in the spring, and three in the autumn. Wolf proposed that people should live forever, but Coyote returned just then and changed this. He said, "We will grow old and die." He went to his house for tobacco, and finding his son sick and dying, he hurried back and cried, "I thought you said we would not die!" "No," answered Wolf, "you insisted that we die, and so it shall be." Coyote's son was the first person to die. ✿

79. A NORTHERN DIEGUEÑO TYPE

80. CHIEF JOSEPH—NEZ PERCE

The Woman in the Fish-skin Parka (*Nunivak*)

A MAN, HIS WIFE, AND FIVE SONS LIVED BY THEMSELVES. The wife combed only half of her hair, allowing the remainder to fall unkemptly over her eyes. The man was a great hunter, but when his sons had grown and had been taught the lore of the chase, he chose to remain at home. One time, when all the sons had gone hunting, two of them failed to return. A long search revealed no sign of them. The following spring two more disappeared, never to come back. Now the father and the youngest son hunted for the family. On a trip where they were forced to stay overnight and had made camp on solid ice, a woman, travel-stained and wearing a fish-skin parka, came up to them and said: "You have worried about your sons. I have come for you. Immediately father and son became unconscious. When they awoke they saw a village near by, but there was no sign of the woman with the fish-skin parka. They approached the village and entered a house, where a woman greeted them: "You will suffer for coming here. Your sons would have been killed long ago, but I kept them alive so that you could them before they died. There they are on that sleeping bench." Father and son saw the others, bodies scratched and emaciated, barely able to move, side by side on the bench. During this time the man's wife was alone. All winter and all spring she waited for the return of her husband and sons. One day a woman wearing a fish-skin parka entered her house, and said, "Your sons, who are very ill, sent me for you." The wife then became unconscious. She awoke in a strange village. She entered the first house, which was that of a woman, who spoke: "Now that you are here, you will suffer. Your husband and sons are nearly dead, but I have kept them alive, so that some day they can help me. The woman in the fish-skin parka caused their suffering." The wife replied: "I did not know what was happening. If I had known, I could have brought along my wooden dish." "You stay here. I shall go for your dish," she answered. Soon the woman returned with the dish. Then the wife said, "I shall go to the men's house and try to save my husband and sons." In the men's house she saw her husband and sons, bodies scratched and emaciated, barely able to stand. All about the room were people, and opposite the entrance was the woman with the fish-skin parka. The wife placed the dish in the middle of the floor, and said: " I am poor. I cannot do much, but I want you people to listen to my song: Eya! Eya! I cannot see that woman's uncle. Can I see that woman's uncle? With my own eyes shall I see him. At the end of her song, she tossed back her unkempt hair, so that her whole face could be seen. She stared hard at all the people, and so intense was her gaze that they caught fire and burned up. The woman with the fish-skin parka was the last to burn. Then the wife killed all the people in the village. She and the woman cared for and fed the man and his sons until they were able to travel. After walking many days, they came to a graveyard, where the woman, who was guiding them, said: "We must go down through that graveyard to reach your home. The evil woman in the fish-skin parka brought you up here through the graveyard. The spirits of people, after death, go up into the middle of the sky, where they travel about." The woman married one of the sons and obtained widows for the others. All lived together in one place. ✿

The Story of Yumuk (*King Island Eskimo*)

YUMUK HAD FULL POSSESSION of all his mental faculties from the moment of conception. He was aware of all that was happening in his mother's womb and while being born. Yumuk had no eyebrows, and his mother, ashamed of him, tattooed them on him. He was so conscious of his lack of eyebrows that, when grown and while traveling from village to village, he feared the ridicule of the people. Sometimes he returned to King island. Once while hunting with a companion, he speared a walrus. The two then lashed together their kayaks, preparatory to cutting up the carcass. The walrus, still alive, pulled Yumuk out of the kayak with his tusks. The man circled about, waiting for the body to come up. Soon Yumuk stuck his head above the surface and called: "I am all right! Do not cry for me! I am safe!" His companion pulled him aboard, and together they killed the walrus. They raised its head so that it would bleed in the kaiak. The blood almost filled the boat. One winter, when Yumuk had gone to Siberia, two youths, disregarding the warnings of relatives, tore down his house to use for firewood. Yumuk, returning and learning who had destroyed his home, thought of revenge. One youth he found sitting on the men's house, arms folded under his parka. The young man, seeing Yumuk and feeling guilty, fled, but Yumuk pursued and stabbed him with a stone knife. Yumuk remained in a house all winter, afraid to come out because the youth's relatives were watching and waiting to kill or starve him. Sometimes a friend smuggled in food, but Yumuk knew that he would not starve, because he was becoming a medicine man. One day he put on the clothing of his friend and walked out unharmed, because if the people killed him thus dressed, it would be as if they had slain the friend against whom they had no feud. Yumuk, when ill, appeared as if about to die, but, after talking to the air, he always became well. One day when very ill he said to his children: "I am tired of living. I am going to die to rest. Look in my grave after four days. I am going to my people. If my body is not there, you will never see me again. Never name a child after me." After four days the children opened the grave, but, finding no body, they knew that he had gone somewhere. Some people on the mainland named a child after Yumuk. Soon it died, and medicine men declared that Yumuk had taken its life. One day, a medicine man, while doctoring, saw Yumuk holding the child. He spoke: "I took the child. If the parents will name another child after me, I shall return this one." When another had been named for him, the spirit returned to the first child, and it lived. The children of Yumuk learned that his spirit had gone somewhere north on the mainland and that people there named their children after Yumuk to keep them from dying. ✿

Titles of illustrations appear in *italics*.